Introductio

Introduction to Insurance

G. C. A. DICKSON
M.Litt., Ph.D., F.C.I.I.

Senior Lecturer, Risk Management
Glasgow College of Technology

J. T. STEELE
B.A., F.C.I.I.

Head of Department, Banking
and Insurance Studies
Glasgow College of Technology

SECOND EDITION

Pitman

Pitman Publishing
128 Long Acre, London WC2E 9AN

A Division of Longman Group UK Ltd

© Macdonald and Evans Ltd 1984

Second edition first published in Great Britain 1984
Reprinted by Pitman Publishing 1986, 1988, 1989, 1991

British Library Cataloguing in Publication Data
Dickson, G. C. A.
   Introduction to insurance. – 2nd ed. –
   1. Insurance
   I. Title   II. Steele, J. T.   III. Dickson, G. C. A.
   Elements of Insurance
   368   HG8051

ISBN 0 273 02790 5

Printed and bound in Singapore

Preface to the Second Edition

This book is aimed primarily at two groups of student readers, those studying the BTEC Option Module "Elements of Insurance" and those involved with the Chartered Insurance Institute examinations. The book embraces the entire BTEC syllabus and the CII "Introduction to Insurance" syllabus, while going some way towards meeting the needs of those who are studying the CII "Principles and Practice of Insurance".

Revision tests in the form of self-assessment questions have been included at the end of each chapter and readers should satisfy themselves that they can answer them before moving on. Halfway through the book and again at the end there are a number of examination questions which require fuller answers than the self-assessment questions. These examination questions should also provide some practice in the type of question which might be expected in an examination.

In our view the book will also be useful to anyone, examination student or otherwise, who is seeking an introduction to the complex but fascinating world of insurance.

No book is written without sacrifices and help from others, and we would like to thank the British Insurance Association, the British Insurance Brokers' Association, Lloyd's of London and the Department of Trade and Industry. Thanks also are due to Professor Hugh Cockerell, City University, London for helpful comments on the first edition of this book published in 1981. Finally our families are thanked for their patience and assistance throughout.

Glasgow
June 1984

G.C.A.D.
J.T.S.

Contents

List of Illustrations

Table of Cases

Table of Statutes

CHAPTER ONE

The Nature of Risk

CHAPTER OBJECTIVES

After studying this chapter you should be able to:
* explain the meanings of and distinguish between the terms chance, probability, uncertainty and risk;
* define and distinguish between (*a*) pure and speculative risks and (*b*) fundamental and particular risks;
* recognise the common features of insurable risks;
* recognise the importance of loss prevention and describe the different approaches to reduction of risk;
* outline the basic principles of risk management.

THE CONCEPT OF RISK

"Although it looks as if it will rain, I think I will take the risk of going out without a coat today." "It's too risky to dive so deep without breathing apparatus." "Drive faster than 30 m.p.h. if you like but you run the risk of being stopped by the police." "I wonder what the risk is of my house being hit by a piece of falling spacecraft?"

What do we mean when we use the word "risk"? It is one of those words that is capable of a number of interpretations and seems to fit in to whatever context it finds itself. Risk is central to the study of insurance and to avoid any ambiguities that may arise in this study, it is as well that we begin by looking at the concept of risk.

Definitions of risk

Risk has been the subject of study by scholars for many centuries and a great deal of thought and effort has gone into defining the concept. While these discussions are of great interest to those concerned with the broader issues of risk we can avoid much of the debate as we wish to concentrate on risk as a foundation to our study of insurance.

It is not possible to be dogmatic and state a definition of risk that is authoritative in the sense that it will find universal acceptance. It is possible, however, to provide a definition that will satisfy our requirement.

We will look upon risk as the uncertainty of loss. This definition avoids situations where no likelihood of loss exists and in the context of the examples at the start of this chapter we could say that the uncertainty of loss, in each one respectively, was the prospect of damaged clothing, personal injury, financial loss by being fined, and property damage.

Taking a more usual example of fire damage to a factory, the owner runs the risk of such damage every day of the week. There is an uncertainty of loss. He experiences this uncertainty on two accounts. First he does not know if and when the loss will occur, and secondly he does not know how severe the loss will be once it has occurred. In a very large factory we could add another uncertainty in that the owner does not know at which part of the factory the loss will occur.

Uncertainty and certainty

This sense of uncertainty surrounds everything we do in life. We do not know if we will pass our exams, if we will succeed in the job interview, if we will gain promotion and so on. In a business sense uncertainty is no less important.

Almost everything the business man does he does in an uncertain environment. If he invests in new machinery, will the output be what is expected, will the employees be prepared to work with it? If he launches a new product will it sell as expected? Will a new bonus scheme for employees avoid a threatened strike? If he builds a new factory will it burn down? Will thieves steal his finished products from the warehouse?

In a few cases he knows, with certainty, what the future holds. He knows if he reduces the number of machines used that his fuel bill will come down. If he employs four new people he knows that his payroll will increase. Most of his activities, however, still involve him in venturing forward in this atmosphere of uncertainty.

It is valuable that we recognise, at this early stage, the omnipresent nature of uncertainty and that, faced with uncertainty, life both personal and business continues day by day.

The measurement of risk

The fact that uncertainty of loss abounds has resulted in a great deal of effort being devoted to the measurement of risk. In measuring risk we are really trying to place some value on our belief as to the likelihood that some event will or will not take place. This evaluation of likelihood attempts to quantify the degree of uncertainty that surrounds the loss.

Probability theory

The most common form of measurement is found in probability theory. There are many different views of probability but in essence it is a means of measuring likelihood along a scale ranging from 0 to 1. In this way we can say that the probability of getting a head from the toss of a fair coin is 0.5; that is, we are equally likely to get a head as we are a tail.

Probability theory is assuming an increasingly important role in insurance but one major problem is that probabilities have, normally, to be based on some past experience. In very many situations there is no such experience and probability calculations are more by way of "guesstimates" about the future.

Psychological aspects of risk
This problem of the lack of past statistics is only one side of a very complex problem. Regardless of whether previous statistics are available there is one other very important aspect in the measurement of risk and that is the attitude which different people have to the same situation.

This can be shown easily by considering a gamble where one person flips a coin. If the coin lands heads up he will pay you £10 but if it lands tails up you must pay him £5. Think about this very carefully and then ask others to do the same. It is unlikely that everyone you ask would agree to gamble on those terms. One factor that will affect our attitude is the amount of money we have to start with. The wealthy person may not mind gambling but if you had only £5 and you had reserved this for something essential you may dislike the gamble.

Take another brief example. Let us say that your friend has flipped a coin and has had twelve heads in a row. Would you still gamble—remember you must pay him £5 if the next flip results in a tail. Based on so many heads in a row the "chances" would seem to be that the next throw will be a tail and most would prefer not to gamble. However, we had said earlier that the probability of getting a tail is 0.5, and this is still so, despite how many previous flips there have been. A person's reaction to this situation is an interesting one, as it tells us that even when probabilities exist to help us, we often assign our own measure of likelihood.

These two factors—our view of money based on our own wealth and our view of likelihood—represent the main psychological aspects of risk measurement and go a long way to explaining the desire for insurance, as we shall see.

Frequency and severity
What do we mean when we say that some event is very risky? Following our definition we could expand this to say that there is a high level of uncertainty of loss. Whether we use the former or the latter there is still some confusion in meaning.

Take as an example the risk of fire damage in a storeroom at a factory. A person may refer to the prospect of fire damage as being "very risky", but does he mean that there is a very strong likelihood of a fire or that it is unlikely that there will be a fire but if it happens it will result in a very high financial loss? In other words when we talk of risk we must be clear in our minds that it incorporates both the frequency with which an event may take place and the severity of each incident that does occur.

The operation of a chemical plant is very risky, not because such plants have frequent losses but because when a loss does take place it involves very substantial sums of money. The explosion at the Flixborough plant in 1974 is a good example of this point. The opposite could be the case where a large department store considers the breakage of glass windows to be very risky. They are not referring to the cost of each broken window but to the frequency with which windows are broken and the fact that in aggregate, in total, the cost of broken glass is high.

Chance
Just before leaving the question of risk measurement let us look at the use of the word "chance". This word often appears in the literature when risk is being discussed. People talk of the chance of something happening or some event coming about and we could have substituted "chance" for "uncertainty" in our definition of risk as the uncertainty of loss. There was, however, a good reason for not doing so and it is based on the occasions when people normally use the word "chance".

It would be unlikely for someone to talk about the risk of winning the football pools whereas it is quite normal for people to talk about the chance of winning the pools. In a similar way people normally refer to the risk of unemployment rather than the chance of unemployment. By monitoring when these two words are commonly used we can conclude that chance is reserved normally for those situations where the outcome is desired, e.g. winning the pools, and risk relates to outcomes that are not looked for, e.g. the risk of being unemployed.

In this way it would be strange to talk of the chance of loss in the context of, say, fire damage and more appropriate to refer to this as the risk of damage, or as we have defined it the uncertainty of loss.

FORMS OF RISK

The emphasis on the word "loss" in our definition of risk highlights the fact that we are concerned with those risks that hold out the prospect of some loss that is capable of financial measurement. With this in mind we can discuss two separate dichotomies of risk.

Pure and speculative
We have looked at the pervasive nature of risk in both private and business contexts but even when we have limited our study of risk to

those situations that involve a potential loss there is one further distinction that must be made. To have a situation that involves a loss we could imagine two combinations of situations.

The first form of situation holding out the prospect of a loss could be where both a loss or a break-even position may materialise. Driving a motor car represents an example of this. Every time you take your car on the road you run a risk—there is the uncertainty of loss. You may damage your car or other property or incur a liability because of injury sustained by someone. Should you get home free of incident then we could say you have broken even.

The second situation is where you may experience a loss, break even, or make a profit. A good example of this kind of risk is evidenced by the stock market and those who buy shares. You may purchase shares at 25p each and a year later they may only be worth 20p. On the other hand they may not have changed value and could still stand at 25p. What you hope, of course, is that they have risen in price and when you want to sell them you will profit by the sale.

These two types of event are termed respectively pure and speculative risks. A pure risk holds out the prospect of a loss or no loss while a speculative risk holds out the prospect of a gain as well as loss or break-even.

In the business world speculative risks are very common. Exporting to a new market, launching a new product and fixing retail prices are all forms of speculative risk as they hold out the prospect of loss, break-even or profit. Pure risks are equally common. The factory may burn down, profit may be lost following a fire, money may be stolen. These situations hold out the prospect of loss but at the same time they may not occur and the result will be that the status quo will be maintained. It is important to realise that the firm does not gain solely through the fact that the factory did not burn, that profit was not lost following a fire or that money was not stolen, it simply maintains the status quo or, as we have said earlier, has broken even.

Fundamental and particular

A further method of classifying risks is to divide them into fundamental and particular. A fundamental risk is one that is impersonal both in origin and consequence. The losses that flow from fundamental risks are not normally caused by one individual and their impact generally falls on a wide range of people.

Rather than talk of fundamental risks it may be helpful to refer to risks of a fundamental nature. They are termed "fundamental" as they arise out of the nature of the society we live in or from some physical occurrence beyond the control of man. Examples of such risks are war, inflation, changing customs, typhoons and tidal waves, the first three arising out of the kind of society we have and the last two being attributable to some physical occurrence.

A particular risk, or a risk of a particular nature, has its origin in individual events and its impact is felt locally. Theft of property, accidental damage to personal effects and explosion of a boiler are examples of pure risks.

Changes in classifications

Attitudes change over time and there are examples of risks moving from one classification to another. The most common alteration in classification has been from particular to fundamental and this fact does give some hint as to why we bother to classify risks at all. Before looking at this question let us take two examples of risks changing classification.

Unemployment, at one time, was looked upon as the fault of the individual concerned. It may have arisen out of his laziness, lack of training or a host of reasons but unemployment was very much a particular risk. Over many years the view of society has changed and today most people would agree that unemployment arises out of some malfunctioning of the economic system. In this way the risk has changed to be one of a fundamental nature, not attributable to any one individual and widespread in its consequences.

Motor accidents represent another area of risk where changes are taking place. The popular view for a long time has been that a motor accident is brought about by the fault of one person and the legal systems in most countries acknowledge this by having a system of compensation that relies on the person who has suffered injury, or who has had property damaged, proving that the driver was to blame. Gradually, however, this view is altering and some people are beginning to wonder if it would not be more accurate to think of the motor accident as having arisen due to a combination of events, not all of which are within the control of the driver. Evidence of this change is found in those countries where state compensation exists without proof of fault.

These two examples do, as indicated earlier, provide some clue as to why it is necessary to have the particular and fundamental dichotomy. When a risk is looked upon as being of a fundamental nature the government has normally taken notice of the views of society and stepped in with some scheme to provide compensation for victims, for example, by means of unemployment benefit.

INSURABLE RISKS

So far we have talked of risk in a very general way using a wide range of examples. As we said earlier a study of risk is to be a foundation for a more detailed examination of insurance and so we must now turn our attention to those risks that can be insured. Insurable risks have certain common features, including those shown in the following list, and as your study progresses you should be able to identify those risks that are and are not capable of being insured.

Financial value
The risk must involve a loss that is capable of financial measurement. We have touched on this before and it is important to remember that insurance is concerned only with situations where monetary compensation is given following a loss. This feature of the insurable risk is easily identified in, for example, damage to property where the level of compensation can be equated with the cost of repairs.

In life assurance it is rather more difficult to say that the financial loss suffered by a wife when her husband dies is a specific sum of money. What we can say is that the level of compensation to be paid in the event of death has been determined prior to taking out the policy.

Homogeneous exposures
There must be a large number of similar, homogeneous risks before any one of that number is capable of being insured. There are two reasons for this. The first is that, as we have noted already, the measurement of risk by probabilities and statistics relies on there being a reasonable experience of past events. The second is that if there were only three or four exposures then each one would have to contribute a very high amount if losses were to be met from these contributions. On the other hand if there were thousands of similar exposures then the contributions could be comparatively small as only a few would be unfortunate enough to suffer a loss and hence require it to be met from the contribution. The insurance of household contents against fire is an example of homogeneous exposures whereas the insurance of a concert pianist's fingers is not.

Pure risks only
Insurance is concerned only with pure risks; speculative risks, where there is the possibility of some gain, cannot be insured. This is generally the case although certain modern developments may lead us to alter this statement in due course. Speculative risks are normally taken in the hope of a gain and the provision of insurance may act as a distinct disincentive to effort in that even if you do not try as hard as you could to bring about the gain you will still earn the profit from your insurance policy. This is obviously not acceptable but in addition the speculative risk can often be unacceptable for other reasons such as lack of

statistical experience or high probability of a loss on the part of the insurer.

It is important to note that we are not concluding that all pure risks are insurable; what we are saying is that speculative risks, on the whole, are not.

Particular and fundamental risks

Particular risks are generally insurable provided they satisfy the other criteria of insurable risks. Fundamental risks, however, do not present such a straightforward picture. The widespread, indiscriminate nature of the effect of most fundamental risks has resulted in them traditionally being uninsurable. It is not accurate to say that all fundamental risks cannot be insured but it is true to say that insurers are very careful in selecting those for which they wish to provide cover.

Fundamental risks that arise out of the nature of the society we live in are largely uninsurable and those that arise due to some physical occurrence depend for their insurability on the circumstances.

Fortuitous

The loss must be entirely fortuitous as far as the person seeking insurance is concerned. It is not possible to insure against an event that will occur with certainty, as in such a case there would be no risk, no uncertainty of loss. The frequency and severity of any risk must be completely beyond the control of the person insuring.

In the case of most risks this will always be apparent but in life assurance some could argue that there is no uncertainty about death: it is one of the few certainties we have. Life assurance is, however, still involved with fortuitous events as it is the *timing* of death that is beyond the control of the person effecting the policy. This is not true in the case of suicide and most policies will cover death from suicide as long as it occurs a reasonable time after the policy was taken out, i.e. suicide was not being planned—at least not in the short term—when the policy was effected.

Insurable interest

The risk that is to be insured must result in some form of financial loss and it is easy to anticipate situations where a person could insure some other person's house or car so that when the house or car was damaged he, in addition to the owner of the property, would receive compensation from the insurance company. To take this thought a stage further there would be no reason why a person could not go round the local hospital and take out a life assurance policy on the lives of those people who were very ill.

To counteract this possibility one of the basic doctrines of insurance is that the person insuring must be the one who stands to suffer some financial loss if the risk materialises. We will return to this topic in Chapter Eight.

Not against public policy

It is a common principle in law that contracts must not be contrary to what society considers the right and moral thing to do. This applies to insurance contracts in the same way and one form of risk that is not insurable is one that is against public policy. It would not be acceptable to society at large, for instance, if a person could burn down his own factory or shop in order to recover insurance money and this form of risk has been catered for above when we said that the loss must be fortuitous as far as the person insuring is concerned.

One form of risk not mentioned earlier was the risk of being fined by the police. The fine is intended to penalise the person and while insurance may be available to meet the losses following, say, a motor accident it is not possible to provide insurance to pay the fine of the driver who was found guilty of some offence.

Reasonable premium

The final feature of the insurable risk is that the premium must be seen to be reasonable in relation to the likely financial loss. A risk that results in a loss with an extremely high frequency may involve a premium that would be unreasonable from the insuring person's point of view. Similarly a straightforward risk such as that caused by fire or theft may result in an unreasonable premium depending upon the object exposed. The insurance premium required to cover a ball point pen against fire or theft may be quite unreasonable in relation to the potential financial loss in view of the insurance companies' costs.

LOSS PREVENTION

The picture being built up is one of an environment in which risk is invariably present in one form or another. In spite of this life continues on both a personal and a business level but the pervasive nature of risk has resulted in a great deal of effort being directed at how losses can be prevented.

Loss prevention is sometimes referred to as risk reduction but we can look upon the terms as being synonymous. Our definition of risk was uncertainty of loss and risk reduction can therefore be viewed as a means of removing some or all of this uncertainty.

The importance of loss prevention cannot be understated. In 1983 fires caused damage in Great Britain estimated at £565.6 million. This is an extremely high figure and it is difficult to visualise what it actually means. The amount refers to fire damage, whether insured or not, but does not include other losses—such as lost profit—that flow from a fire. To try and put this figure, sometimes known as the fire waste figure, in perspective we could say that on average over the whole of 1983 fire damage cost almost £18 every single *second* of the year.

To reduce this high fire loss figure would be commendable on its own and certainly sufficient justification for examining methods of loss prevention but what makes these efforts all the more necessary is the fact that the loss does not end with the visible damage. Just as we noted above, fire damage results in a chain of other losses and this is true for most forms of risk.

Let us look at one risk as an example. A pure and particular risk to which almost all businesses are exposed is the one of injury to employees. When an employee is injured he may succeed in legal action against his employer for compensation and the employer will have an insurance policy to provide him with the money he requires to pay the injured employee's claim. The claim from the employee can be looked upon in the same way as the fire damage cost: it is not the end of the story. At the time of the injury there will have been a stoppage of production and other employees may have to act as witnesses at a court case if one ensues. While the injured man is away from work there will be lost production, and another person may have to be trained to take his place. The point is that if the loss could have been prevented it would have resulted in there being no injury and no consequential stream of losses. The importance of loss prevention goes beyond the individual or firm involved in the loss as the whole of society benefits from there being fewer losses in the long run.

Elimination

Many people equate loss prevention with elimination of loss. This is natural enough as one sure way of not having a loss is to eliminate the possibilty altogether.

In a domestic sense this can often be done. Where a person is really concerned over the likelihood of a motor accident then he or she could sell their car and eliminate the risk. In the same way they may be alarmed in case their pet dog causes injury to neighbouring children and they could sell or otherwise dispose of the animal in order to eliminate the risk. For some risks, elimination will not be possible. No matter how worried you may be about the chip pan catching fire in the kitchen you may like chips too much to dispose of the pan. On a more serious note you may be concerned over the possibility of fire damage to your house but you would not think of selling your house to eliminate the risk.

In the business world it is very common to be faced with problems posed by risk where elimination is not possible. There may be considerable risk attached to the building of a new factory, risks that could be eliminated if you decided not to build, but the whole organisation depends upon the new building being constructed and it is just not possible to eliminate the risk entirely.

Minimisation

These thoughts on the inability to eliminate risk lead us on to consider how best the risk or loss can be minimised. Loss prevention is therefore concerned primarily with minimising risk, or according to our definition with minimising the uncertainty of loss. The effort of minimising losses falls into two divisions: pre- and post-loss minimisation.

Pre-loss minimisation

As we will see in Chapter Three insurance companies employ specialists who can assist individuals or firms in working out ways of minimising losses by steps taken before the adverse event has occurred. The wearing of seat belts is a good example of pre-loss minimisation. The essence of this pre-loss minimisation is that the effect of the loss is anticipated and steps taken to ensure that the frequency and/or severity are reduced to the minimum.

The use of guards on dangerous machinery anticipates the risk of injury to employees, the installation of extractor fans in a paint spraying booth anticipates the risks of injury to health and also the possibility of fire damage.

A great measure of experience is required in being able to anticipate risks and persuade people to take steps to minimise their effect. A general response to risk reduction suggestions is the statement "It won't happen to me!" In some cases this is often shown to be sadly inaccurate.

Post-loss minimisation

Even after the risk has materialised and the loss has taken place there are still steps that can be taken to minimise loss. The most common area where post-loss minimisation occurs is probably after fire damage. Property can often be saved from burning buildings and other property salvaged and sold in an attempt to minimise the loss.

Just as pre-loss minimisation anticipated the loss before it took place, post-loss minimisation imagines that the loss has occurred and anticipates a way in which its effect can be minimised. In this way the employment of an industrial nurse may minimise the effect of an injury. Automatic sprinkler installations will minimise the effect of fires.

RISK MANAGEMENT

The term "risk management" is one that has become more and more popular in Great Britain and refers to the overall, corporate approach to problems posed by risk in a business setting.

It is sometimes difficult for those not directly concerned with insurance to realise the importance of it to the business. In some cases the amount spent on insurance premiums each year can run into millions of pounds. With this kind of cost it is not unnatural that firms are beginning to employ their own insurance specialists. Today very many companies have insurance departments and employ highly skilled insurance managers.

The change from insurance to risk management has been taking place gradually over the last two decades as insurance managers realised that their companies were exposed to risk in a far wider sense than that capable of being insured. As we saw earlier only certain pure risks are insurable and even after having insured there will be terms, conditions and exceptions on policies.

Risk management takes a broader view of the problems of risk and can be divided into three main areas, identification, evaluation and control.

Risk identification

Risk management takes the view that a firm is exposed to risk in a variety of ways and any one such way may cause financial loss. Risk is viewed therefore in its widest sense, not limited to those risks that can be insured, and steps are taken, using established risk identification aids, to highlight all areas where a company is likely to suffer. The advantage of having a risk manager identify exposure areas is, in the main, that he is a specialist at his job and is not limited to one particular function of the company. An engineer may be able to identify risks in his area, the lawyer in his and the marketing man in his, but the risk manager has the capability of overseeing all their activities and while not being a specialist in other disciplines he is a specialist in risk.

Evaluation

The second stage in the risk management process is the evaluation of risk or the measurement of its impact on the firm. This involves compiling very accurate records of past events in order that decisions taken in the future are taken on the basis of sound statistics.

The risk manager will have information fed back to him from various sources on such matters as injuries to employees, thefts, storm damage, fires and a host of other risks. With this information he can calculate the frequency and severity with which certain events occur and will be in a better position to determine how best to handle the risks that are posed.

One very important reason for carrying out careful evaluation is to ensure that the company does not spend too much on controlling a risk that is not likely to cost a great deal should the event materialise.

Control

The final step in the process is the control of risk and following on from the evaluation we can now add that we are concerned with the *economic* control of risk. We have dealt with loss prevention and this is an arm of control but what we have not looked at are the ways in which risks can be reduced by some financial mechanism. We could divide this form of risk reduction into the two techniques of retention and transfer.

Retention

Having identified and evaluated a risk the risk manager may decide that his company should retain it and provide for the day when it may materialise by building up a fund of money out of which the loss will be met. This method of risk financing requires a good deal of expertise as the company could suffer a very substantial loss if the fund is not sufficient or the risk has been undervalued. This topic is discussed further in Chapter Five.

One development of the retention of risk has been the formation of captive insurance companies. Certain businesses are so large that they can very well insure some of their risks themselves and in this way save the element of the premiums that would otherwise go towards the insurance companies' costs and expenses. A wholly-owned subsidiary is set up and some risks are passed to it with the premiums paid by the parent organisation. In some cases the captive also transacts insurance for firms other than its parent and can very often become a profit-maker in the same way as any other subsidiary that the parent may establish.

Transfer

The second method of financial risk control could be said to be those situations where the company transfers the effect of the loss to some other person or company. A company that owns property and lets it out to tenants is exposed to the risk that their property may be damaged by fire. The company can transfer this risk by writing into the lease that the tenant is responsible for fire damage and must effect a fire insurance policy. This is looked upon as financial risk control as the owners of the property are, in a sense, paying to have the risk transferred: if they had retained the risk they could probably have charged a higher rent.

The most common form of risk transfer is by way of insurance and in Chapter Three we will go on to examine the function of insurance as a risk-transfer mechanism.

SELF-ASSESSMENT QUESTIONS

Select the correct option or options under each of the questions shown below.

1. (a) Risk is the uncertainty of loss.
   (b) Attitude to risk is the same for everyone.
   (c) The word "chance" is normally reserved for risks where the outcome is desired.
   (d) Risks can be classified as either pure or particular and fundamental or speculative.
2. Some common features of insurable risks are that they:
   (a) do not happen very often;
   (b) must involve a loss that is capable of financial measurement;
   (c) are not to be fortuitous from the insuring person's point of view;
   (d) are not against public policy.
3. Loss prevention is important as:
   (a) risks must be eliminated if businesses are to operate successfully;
   (b) the cost of damage and associated losses is extremely high;
   (c) society benefits from there being few losses.

CHAPTER TWO

The Main Classes of Insurance

CHAPTER OBJECTIVES

After studying this chapter you should be able to:
* distinguish the main classes of insurance as currently classified by statute;
* outline the scope of the main classes of insurance;
* outline the development in the United Kingdom of the main classes of insurance.

INTRODUCTION

As we will see in Chapter Four, insurance business has been divided into seven classes of long term business and seventeen classes of general business, by statute. This is substantially different from the divisions known by many who have spent some years in insurance companies where the traditional division was between fire, marine, accident and life assurance.

The increasing complexities and sophistication of covers expanded these four divisions with some forms of insurance crossing lines of classification. In this chapter we will combine classes and deal with insurance business under seven headings, namely fire and other damage to property, liability, suretyship credit and pecuniary, motor, marine and aviation, accident and health, and life assurance.

The chart in Fig. 1 illustrates the growth of the main forms of insurance and as we come to each type we will examine briefly the historical development before going on to look at the scope of the insurance today. From the illustration you will notice how most forms of insurance started after the industrial revolution.

The use of the word "*insurance*" often related to something which *might* happen, e.g. fire *in*surance; *a*ssurance related to something which *would* happen, e.g. death, and therefore life *a*ssurance. The words insured, assured, insurer and assurer had similar connotations. Today these words are used loosely and no importance is attached to the difference.

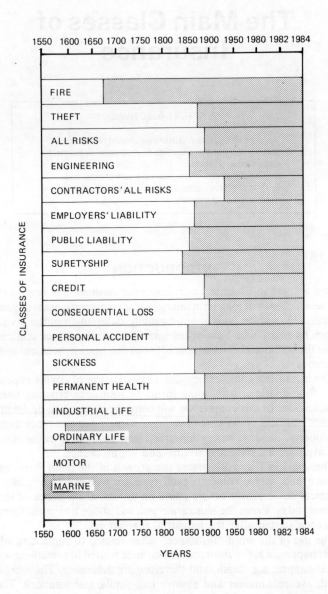

Fig. 1. *The main forms of insurance and their growth rates.* The shaded area shows the commencement date of the various forms of insurance.

FIRE AND OTHER LOSS OF OR DAMAGE TO PROPERTY

Historical perspective

Protection against damage to property has been sought by man from earliest times. Physical protection has always been possible but financial protection became more and more important when towns and villages grew up and people depended on each other for their well-being.

Early records show that compensation in the event of fire was one of the first forms of insurance and losses were normally paid in a charitable way from donations, by guilds of craftsmen or churches. Gradually the need arose for a far more formal means of providing compensation and this came to a head in the case of fire damage after the Great Fire of London in 1666.

Early fire insurance companies

Some early documents provide evidence of the existence of fire insurance in 1667 but the Fire Office, set up in 1680, is generally regarded as being the first fire insurance company. In 1705 the Fire Office changed its name to the Phoenix as this was the symbol represented on the company's fire mark. These fire marks, normally made of metal, bore the insignia of the fire insurance company and were nailed to an outside wall. They performed two very valuable functions. The first was that they were a cheap and prominent form of advertising and the second, of more importance to the owner of the property and thereby providing the incentive to display them, was that they indicated to the fire brigade that the house was insured. It has to be remembered that fire brigades were controlled by, mainly, the insurance companies and each ran independently. It was important therefore to display the fire marks so as to guide the fire brigade to the insured building. Following an abortive attempt at municipal insurance by the Corporation of London during the period 1681–2 a second company, the Friendly Society, was founded in 1683.

The fourth office appropriately titled "The Amicable Contributors for Insuring Houses from Loss by Fire" came along in 1696 and soon became known as the Hand-in-Hand. It transacted business successfully until 1905 when it was absorbed by the Commercial Union. Later companies were the Sun Fire Office (1710), the Union (1714), and the Westminster (1717).

Tooley Street fire

On 22nd June 1861 one of the landmarks in the development of fire insurance took place. A fire broke out in wharves and warehouses along the banks of the Thames near to the centre of London. The fire spread quickly and caused damage costing the fire insurance companies, in aggregate, £1,000,000.

The immediate response was a large increase in premiums charged for this type of property but after representations from city merchants they were modified. Some of the effects resulting from the Tooley Street fire were as follows.

(*a*) The problems of how much to charge for wharves and warehouses was dealt with by a new committee, the London Wharf and Warehouse Committee.

(*b*) Differential rates of charges were adopted in an effort to encourage owners to think about fire precautions. Bad features were penalised and good ones rewarded.

(*c*) The inadequacy of the existing fire fighting forces was highlighted and the Metropolitan Fire Brigade Act 1865 established a fire service for London run by the city itself.

(*d*) Two new companies were formed, the Commercial Union and the Mercantile, later the North British and Mercantile.

Loss of, and non-fire damage to, property

It was some time after the start of fire insurance that attention was turned to non-fire damage but eventually a range of additional or special perils were made available. These perils are detailed later.

One of the other most common forms of loss involving property is theft but it was not until 1887 that the first fire policy was extended to include theft cover. The Mercantile Accident and Guarantee Insurance Company began issuing theft policies in 1889, although the term used then was "burglary". The use of the word "theft" followed on from the Theft Act 1968 when the legal definition of what constituted a theft was given. The Fine Art and General Insurance Company Ltd. in 1890, the Goldsmiths and General Burglary Insurance Association in 1891, and the National Burglary Insurance Corporation in 1892 continued the development of theft insurance as a separate form of business.

Towards the end of the nineteenth century a logical development of fire and theft insurance came about with the introduction of all risks covers. This form of insurance represented a wide form of cover against loss of or damage to property from almost any cause, subject to certain exceptions. This therefore includes both fire, theft and other forms of accidental damage.

Engineering

The changes brought about by the industrial revolution brought with them many problems. One such problem was posed by the risk of damage and injury inherent in the operation of new machinery. The most frequent occurrence in connection with machinery was the explosion of boilers and other pressure plant that was then being employed to power machinery.

Safety standards were little thought of in these early days and it is interesting to note that the development of engineering insurance ran in parallel with the safety inspection of boilers, In 1854 the Steam Boiler Assurance Company began issuing insurance policies combined with an inspection service. Eventually public feeling grew to such an extent that in 1882 the Boiler Explosions Act was passed by which severe penalties could be imposed if the explosion of a boiler was found to have been the fault of the owner. This form of legislation continued and expanded to cover other areas of industrial health and safety and we shall look at some of it later.

Standard fire policy

A standard fire policy is used for almost all business insurances, with Lloyd's of London also issuing a standard fire policy that is slightly different in its wording. The basic intention of the fire policy is to provide compensation to the insured person in the event of there being damage to the property insured.

Insured perils

It is not possible, in the commercial world, to issue a policy that will provide compensation regardless of how the damage occurs. The insurance company, the insurers, have to know the perils they are insuring.

The standard fire policy covers damage to property caused by fire, lightning or explosion, where this explosion is brought about by gas or boilers not used for any industrial purpose. This is limited in its scope and property can be damaged in other ways and to meet this need a number of extra perils, known as "special perils", can be added on to the basic policy. These perils are:

storm tempest or flood	riot, civil commotion
burst pipes	malicious damage
earthquake	explosion
aircraft	impact
subsidence, landslip	sprinkler leakage

It is important to remember that these additional perils must result in damage to the property and it is usual to precede each by saying, "damage to the property caused by . . .".

The property insured

In most commercial policies the insured will require cover for buildings,

machinery and plant, and stock. These are the three main headings under which property is insured and in some cases a list of such items can
run to many pages depending upon the size of the insured company.

Theft insurance

Theft policies have the same aim as the standard fire policy in that they
intend to provide compensation to the insured in the event of loss of the
property insured. The property to be insured, for a commercial venture,
will be the same as under the fire policy except of course for the buildings. The theft policy will, in addition, show a more detailed definition of
the stock. The reason for this is that fire is indiscriminate and a thief is
not, so the insurers charge a greater premium for stock which is attractive to thieves.

The law relating to theft was brought up to date by the Theft Act
1968. This had an immediate impact on insurance companies as it
defined the term "theft". The legal definition was wider than that which
the companies were prepared to offer, especially for business premises,
as the definition did not mention any need for there to be force and
violence in committing a theft. This meant that shop-lifting, for
example, was "theft" and this kind of risk had traditionally been uninsurable. To remedy the problem insurance companies included in
their policies a phrase to the effect that theft, within the meaning of the
policy, was to include force and violence either in breaking into or out of
the premises of the insured.

All risks insurances

Uncertainty of loss is not restricted to events brought about by fire or
theft, nor is it limited to events occurring on or about the insured's premises. This realisation led, as we noted earlier, to the development of a
wider form of cover known as "all risks". The term "all risks" is unfortunate in the sense that it does not provide cover against *all* risks as
there are a number of exceptions, but it is an improvement on the scope
of cover available.

Personal effects

All risks policies are very popular with individuals who seek a wider
protection than that afforded by the policies available to cover
household effects. The all risks policy can be taken out on particularly
expensive items such as jewellery, cameras and fur coats, and can also
be arranged on unspecified goods for a lump sum. The twin objectives
of such policies are to provide cover for the whole range of accidental
loss or damage and to do so wherever the goods themselves happen to
be at the time of loss.

Business all risks

The use of all risks policies in the commercial sector is becoming more popular as expensive and sophisticated pieces of machinery are introduced to the factory and the office. The advent of the microprocessor and the silicon chip means that comparatively small machines, often desk-top equipment, have replaced larger and bulkier apparatus. It is quite easy for a small desk-top computer to be accidentally dropped or otherwise damaged.

Goods-in-transit

This form of cover provides compensation to the owner of goods if the goods are damaged or lost while in transit. Different policies can be taken out depending upon whether the goods are carried by a company's own vehicles or by a firm of carriers. In the same way the carrier can effect a policy as he is often responsible for the goods while they are in his custody. Most undertakings depend to a great extent on the carriage of goods by road and this form of cover is an important aspect of industrial activity.

(We have dealt with goods-in-transit insurance here under the heading of "Damage to property" although according to the latest classification of insurance business by statute it should be handled along with motor, marine or aviation insurances.)

Contractors' all risks

This is one of the newer forms of insurance that has been developed to meet the changing needs of industry. When new buildings or civil engineering projects such as motorways or bridges are being constructed a great deal of money is invested before the work is finished. The risk is that the particular building or bridge may sustain severe damage and this would prolong the construction time and delay the eventual completion date. The risk is all the more acute as the completion date draws near and there are many examples of buildings and other projects sustaining severe damage, and even total destruction, only days before they were due to be handed over to the new owners.

Money insurance

The loss of money represents the final form of all risks cover we will look at. The policy provides compensation to the insured in the event of money being stolen either from his business premises, from his own home or while it is being carried to or from the bank.

One important addition to this cover is often the provision of some compensation to employees who may be injured or have clothing damaged during a robbery.

Glass

Cover is also available against accidental breakage of plate glass in windows and doors. In the case of shops this is often extended to include damage done to shop-window contents.

Engineering

As we saw earlier the provision of engineering cover had its beginnings with boiler explosions. This still forms a major part of the work done by engineering insurers but the increasing sophistication of industry has resulted in policies being required to cover other forms of engineering plant particularly lifts, cranes, electrical equipment, engines and, more recently, computers. The cover is intended to provide compensation to the insured in the event of the plant insured being damaged by some extraneous cause or its own breakdown.

Engineering insurers still continue to provide an inspection service on a wide range of engineering plant and this is a service much sought after by industry not only because many forms of inspection are compulsory by law but because engineering insurers have built up a considerable expertise in this area.

LIABILITY

The development of liability insurance is of more recent origin than fire insurance and certain other forms of insurance in respect of damage to property that we have already looked at.

Historical perspective

The growth in liability insurance can be dealt with under two headings, employers' and public liability.

Employers' liability

Where an employee is injured by the fault of the employer the right arises for that injured person to claim compensation, or "damages", from the employer. Today this fact is accepted as sound and just but it was not so some 150 years ago.

During the early part of the nineteenth century the industrialisation of Britain had brought many people to the towns and cities of the country where work was to be found in the new factories being built everywhere. As has often been portrayed in word and picture these factories were dark, dismal places where men and women spent long hours in hard and exhausting work. Apart from certain enlightened employers, the drive after more and more production resulted in appalling conditions and a disregard for safety, causing many injuries.

The view, in those days, was that an industrial injury was very much a particular risk and not the responsibility of the employer. The principle applying was one known as *volenti non fit injuria* which meant that the employee had consented to run the risk of injury by being employed. In addition to this principle the ordinary employee would have found it extremely difficult to succeed in any claim due to lack of money and poor education. Moreover, the law allowed employers to avoid any liability for injury where the injury was caused in part by the employee himself, no matter how little he may have contributed to it, and also that liability could be avoided where the injury sustained by one employee was caused by another. This latter defence was known as *common employment* of which the judge in the case of *Priestley* v. *Fowler* (1837) said, "What, make a master liable if one of his servants injures another! If this is allowed, where shall we stop?"

Employers' liability legislation

In 1880 the Employers' Liability Act placed certain employees in a much better legal position. Railwaymen, miners, labourers and others now found that they could sue their employers with a slightly higher chance of success, but many of the obstacles mentioned above still persisted. This was also the year in which the first specialist insurer was established, the Employers' Liability Assurance Corporation.

A significant step forward took place with the passing of the Workmen's Compensation Act 1897. This provided scale benefits such as £300 on death and half earnings during disablement up to £1 per week regardless of proof of fault. The Act lasted with alterations until 1946 when the National Insurance (Industrial Injuries) Act took its place.

As yet there was no compulsion on employers to carry insurance to provide the funds out of which claims were to be paid, although talk of compulsory insurance can be traced back to 1897. Compulsory insurance eventually came with the passing of the Employers' Liability (Compulsory Insurance) Act 1969 which was effective from 1st January 1972.

Public liability

Little has been reported on the historical development of public liability insurance, the provision of insurance for legal liability to pay claims to those who are injured but are not employees. The earliest policies, towards the last quarter of the nineteenth century, related to horse drawn coaches and this later developed into motor vehicle insurance of which more will be said later.

Employers' liability insurance

When an employer is held legally liable to pay damages to an injured employee, or the representatives of someone fatally injured, he can claim against his employers' liability policy which will provide him with exactly the same amount he himself has had to pay out. In addition the policy will also pay certain expenses by way of lawyer's fees or doctor's charges where an injured man has been medically examined.

Insurance is compulsory for all but a few employers and this has resulted in employers' liability insurance forming a large part of the insurance transacted in Britain. With each policy an annual certificate is issued which must be displayed at every place of business as evidence of the fact that the employer has complied with the law and effected a policy.

Public liability insurance

The intention of the public liability policy is to do exactly the same for the insured in relation to claims he may have to meet as the employers' liability policy. It is not concerned with injuries to people who are employed by the insured and to this extent can be effected even by a private individual to protect himself against the likelihood of injuring someone or causing damage and having to pay a claim for damages. The common forms of public liability covers are business policies, products liability, professional liability, and personal public liability. Each of these will now be considered in turn.

Business policies. Any member of the public could be injured or have property damaged by the activities of a business and they could then claim damages from the company.

Products liability. An exception on most business public liability policies is one relating to liability arising out of goods sold. This is a very onerous liability and one that insurers would prefer to deal with separately. If a person is injured by any product he purchases, foodstuffs for example, and he can show that the seller, or in some cases the manufacturer, was to blame he could succeed in a claim for damages.

Professional liability. Another exception on the basic public liability policy is one relating to liability arising out of professional negligence. This can arise where lawyers, accountants, doctors, insurance brokers and a whole range of professional men do or say things that result in others suffering in some sense.

Personal public liability. Each individual owes a duty to their neighbour not to cause them injury or damage their property. Liability may arise out of the ownership of a house, a pet, sporting activities or just in the simple act of crossing the road without looking. The case of *Clark* v. *Shepstone* (1968) emphasises the need for personal public liability cover. Mrs. Shepstone stepped from the pavement without looking and caused a motor-cyclist to swerve. The bike crashed and the pillion passenger, Mr. Clark, suffered severe injury. He sued Mrs. Shepstone and eventually accepted £28,500. In the absence of a personal public liability policy Mrs Shepstone would have been in serious financial difficulties.

SURETYSHIP, CREDIT AND PECUNIARY INSURANCES

Historical perspective

The forms of insurance dealt with under this heading are often referred to as pecuniary insurances as they relate to the loss of money, by one means or another, as opposed to damage to property or legal liability.

Suretyship, or fidelity guarantee, insurance caters for the risk of losing money by the fraud or dishonesty of some other person. People who held positions of responsibility often had others act as surety, or in other words as guarantors prepared to refund any money misappropriated by them in the course of their business.

As may be imagined, the provision of these sureties was a very hazardous activity, and in 1840 the Guarantee Society was formed to provide the surety by means of a policy of insurance. Five years later, in 1845, the British Guarantee Society was formed in Edinburgh and began transacting a similar form of business.

Towards the end of the nineteenth century, in 1893, another form of pecuniary insurance began to be transacted by the Excess Insurance Company. This attempted to meet the risk of a purchaser not paying for goods bought. This became known as credit insurance and by 1918 a specialist company, still operating today, was formed called the Trade Indemnity Company. For foreign transactions the government established in 1920 the Export Credit Scheme, now known as the Export Credits Guarantee Department (ECGD).

Suretyship insurances

These forms of fidelity guarantee fall into the four main categories outlined below.

Commercial guarantees. These will be effected by employers in respect of persons who have some position within the company where they may be in a position to perpetrate some form of fraud.

Government guarantees. These are the local government equivalent of the commercial guarantees described above.

Court bonds. Where the court appoints a person to wind up an estate of someone who dies without a will or to handle the affairs of someone who cannot do so for themselves through age, insanity or some other reason, then it often requires a bond to be issued. This bond, a document that must be signed, sealed and delivered, is to cover any financial loss suffered due to the dishonesty or bad management of affairs by the person appointed by the court.

Government bonds. A common example of a government bond is where an accountant is appointed to act in a bankruptcy and the bond refers to any financial loss suffered while he is carrying out his duties as liquidator.

Credit insurances

As was mentioned earlier these insurances refer to the possibilty of the purchaser of goods or services not paying for them as he should. The business is divided between home and export with the export side being handled by the ECGD.

Pecuniary loss insurance

When premises are damaged by fire the payment of insurance monies will greatly relieve the hardship associated with repairs and rebuilding. What has not been mentioned so far are the losses that are the consequence of fire damage: the consequential losses.

Loss of rent

When a building has been damaged, even though damaged enough so that it cannot be used until repairs are carried out, the person occupying the building may still be obliged contractually to pay rent to the owner. In a similar case the owner may lose rent where the tenant has been relieved of the obligation to pay it.

Loss of profits

A more serious aspect of consequential loss is where business premises are damaged and profits are lost while the business is interrupted due to the fire. This interruption period can last in some cases for many years. Not only must the building be rebuilt but customers who may have gone elsewhere for their products must be won back and it may take some time to reach previous sales levels.

During this interruption period there will be a loss of revenue resulting in a loss of net profit, that is the profit after the expenses of production have been deducted. In addition the company may still incur certain standing charges, or fixed costs, that are not reduced due to the fire such as rent, rates, wages and salaries for certain employees, interest on loans, etc. Finally additional expense may be incurred by the company in minimising the loss in revenue through leasing alternative temporary premises.

Legal expenses

A comparatively new form of insurance protection, within the last fifteen years, is the provision of cover for legal expenses. The risk being faced by a person or company is looked upon as being the uncertainty over whether or not legal expenses may be incurred and if incurred what they may amount to. In return for an annual premium the insured person can be freed from this uncertainty as the insurer agrees to meet legal costs subject to certain exceptions.

Cover is available to private individuals and organisations both of whom now face an ever-increasing possibility of legal action. One growing area of cover is among trade unions and professional bodies. Many such organisations offer a legal service as one of the benefits of membership but with escalating costs it is very difficult for them to budget. To ease the problem they can purchase legal expenses insurance and pay a fixed premium each year.

COMBINED AND COMPREHENSIVE POLICIES

Many of the forms of cover already dealt with are required by the same individual or business. A householder who owns and occupies his own house will require fire, special perils, loss of rent and additional expenses (rates, and ground rent in the case of the owner/occupier), theft, glass, money and liability insurances. The industrial purchaser may require the same with the possible addition of goods-in-transit, engineering, fidelity, credit and loss of profits insurances.

Combined insurances
The advantages of combining various forms of insurance into one policy form are the following:

(a) it is less costly from the administrative point of view;
(b) there is one one premium and one renewal date to bother about;
(c) there is less chance of overlooking one form of cover;
(d) such a combination is easier to market as one product rather than several independent policies.

These combined policies, sometimes known as "traders' combined" or "shopkeepers' combined", are very suitable for a large number of business insureds although the larger the insured becomes the greater the need to arrange insurances specially for him.

Comprehensive insurances
A step on from issuing combined polices, which is only the combination of separate policies within the one folder, is the comprehensive policy. This form of cover represents a widening in the scope of cover. This is evidenced by the household comprehensive policy which, in addition to covering the basic perils mentioned above, also includes cover against damage caused by collapse of television aerials, leakage of central heat-

ing oil and the breakage of underground water pipes, sanitary fittings and many more risks. This widening in cover has not been without its problems and many insurers have experienced considerable losses on their household insurance business as a result of which substantial increases in premiums have been introduced.

Comprehensive policies are also available for offices and shops where cover is provided as a package. This is an efficient and relatively inexpensive way to provide cover for small offices and shops.

MOTOR

Historical perspective

The first mechanically propelled motor vehicle appeared on British roads in 1894 and by 1898 the Law Accident and Insurance Society Ltd. were offering policies to motor vehicle owners. The business was new and many of the early companies did not survive in the competition that ensued which reduced rates to uneconomic levels.

The mushrooming use and development of the motor car followed the First World War during which the advantages of motor vehicles had been established. By the 1920s there were so many motor vehicles on the roads that legislation was almost inevitable and in 1930 the Road Traffic Act was passed.

Compulsory insurance

The intention of the 1930 Act, *inter alia,* was to ensure that funds would be available to compensate the innocent victims of motor accidents. This was to be provided by means of insurance against legal liability to pay damages to injured persons.

The insurance requirement applied to all users of motor vehicles except where some special legal arrangement was in force. Further legislation followed in the Road Traffic Act 1960 and the Motor Vehicles (Passenger Insurance) Act 1972, so that today insurance must be in force to cover legal liability to pay damages to any person, including others in the car, arising out of injury.

Types of motor insurance

Private car insurance

The minimum requirement by law is to provide insurance in respect of legal liability to pay damages arising out of injury caused to any person. A policy for this risk only is available and is termed an "Act only" policy. Such policies are not at all common and are usually reserved for a situation where the risk is exceptionally high. A "third party only" policy would satisfy the minimum legal requirements and in addition would include cover for legal liability where damage was caused to some other person's property. An addition to this form of cover is where damage to the car itself from fire or theft is included, the familiar "third party, fire and theft" policy.

The most popular form of cover, accounting for about 66 per cent of all private car policies, is the "comprehensive policy". It covers all that has been said above with the addition of loss of or damage to the car itself. This policy also includes certain personal accident benefits for the insured and in some cases the insured's spouse. It also provides cover for loss of or damage to personal effects and medical expenses for passengers in the car.

Commercial vehicle policies
All vehicles used for commercial purposes, lorries, taxis, vans, hire cars, milk floats, police cars, etc, are not insured under private car policies but under special contracts known as commercial vehicle policies.

Motorcycles
This is a growing sector of motor insurance business and may well continue to be so if petrol becomes more and more expensive. The type of policy depends upon the machine, whether it is a moped or a high-powered motorbike, and on the age and experience of the cyclist. The cover is comparatively inexpensive relative to motor car insurance.

Motor trade
Special policies are offered to garages and other people within the motor trade to ensure that their liability is covered while using vehicles on the road. Damage to vehicles in garages and showrooms can also be included under such policies.

Special types
The present classification of insurance business refers to "land vehicles other than railway rolling stock" and many such vehicles fall under a category known to insurers as "special types". These will include forklift trucks, mobile cranes, bulldozers and excavators. Such vehicles may travel on roads as well as building sites and other private ground. Where special type vehicles are not used on roads, and are transported from site to site, it is more appropriate to insure the liability under a public liability policy as the vehicle is really being used as a "tool of trade" rather than a motor vehicle.

MARINE AND AVIATION

Historical perspective
Much of the development of marine insurance is dealt with in Chapter

Five where the history of Lloyd's is discussed. Traders from earliest times have protected their ships and cargoes by some form of insurance but the merchants from northern Italy in the twelfth century paid particular attention to this. The early forms of insurance that these and other traders brought to Britain were quite different from what we are used to now.

The bottomry and respondentia bonds involved loans to ship owners or masters where repayment of the loan was not sought if the vessel or cargo respectively did not survive the voyage. The problem with this, and its dissimilarity to present insurance, is that the uncertainty of loss was not removed from the merchant. The ship might still be lost and he would suffer.

London is now the world centre of marine insurance and it is interesting that its introduction to Britain was by the Lombards, merchants who came from northern Italy in the fourteenth and fifteenth centuries. The practice of marine insurance grew quite considerably in these centuries and by 1575 the need was felt for some formalisation of the provision of marine policies and the Chamber of Assurances was established whereby every policy had to be registered. The effect of the Chamber was the introduction of a standardised policy—which has survived almost unaltered to this day—a reduction in the number of disputes arising over cover and the existence of policies; it also gave an air of formality and permanence to marine insurance that had long been lacking. Twenty-six years later in 1601 the Court of Arbitration was established to consider disputes on marine policies; it met in the Chamber of Assurances.

Chartered companies' monopoly

In 1720 the London Assurance and the Royal Exchange Assurance were granted Royal charters to transact marine insurance. The Act providing for the incorporation of the two companies, the Bubble Act, also restricted the provision of marine insurance to these two companies or to individuals. In other words the two companies had almost gained a monopoly. Apart from them only individuals could provide marine insurance, so it is little wonder that the activities in Edward Lloyd's coffee house prospered and, as we will find in Chapter Five, Lloyd's has developed as a market place for insurance provided by individuals.

The virtual monopoly was terminated eventually in 1824 when the Alliance Marine Insurance Company was successful in an application to provide marine insurance.

Marine Insurance Act 1906

The case law that was being accumulated over the years, some 2,000 cases, was incorporated in the Marine Insurance Act 1906 when the law relating to marine insurance was codified and brought together in one statute. The Act forms the basis for the operation of marine insurance to this day and a knowledge of its terms is essential to anyone embarking upon a career in marine insurance. Its value goes beyond the boundary of marine insurance as it is the only code of commercial insurance on the statute book and for that reason is of considerable importance in its own right.

Aviation insurance

The development of aviation insurance is rather easier to record in view of its comparatively recent origins. As with the motor car it was the First World War that highlighted the value of planes and air transport. In 1919 the first regular civil aviation service started but it was not until 1923 that the British Aviation Insurance Group, representing a group formed by the Union of Canton Insurance Company and the White Cross Insurance Association, began offering aviation insurance. This group changed its name twice and by 1936 was known as the Aviation and General Insurance Co. Ltd. Lloyd's syndicates played a major role in the provision of aviation insurance and today much of the business is placed with them.

Marine insurance

Marine policies relate to three areas of risk: the hull, cargo and freight. The risks against which these items are normally insured are collectively termed "perils of the sea" and include fire, theft, collision and a wide range of other perils. While hull and cargo are self explanatory the word "freight" may not be. Freight is the sum paid for transporting goods or for the hire of a ship. When goods are lost by "marine perils" then freight, or part of it, is lost—hence the need for cover.

Forms of policy

The various forms of policy are as follows:

(a) *Time policy.* This is for a fixed period usually not exceeding twelve months.

(b) *Voyage policy.* Operative for the period of the voyage. For cargo the cover is from warehouse to warehouse.

(c) *Mixed policy.* Covers the subject matter for the voyage and a period of time thereafter, e.g. while in port.

(d) *Building risk policy.* Covers the construction of marine vessels.

(e) *Floating policy.* This provides the policyholder with a large reserve of cover for cargo. A large initial sum is granted and each time shipments are sent the insured declares this and the value of the shipment is deducted from the outstanding sum insured.

(f) *Small craft.* The increasing leisure use of small boats brought about the introduction of a policy aimed at this form of craft. It is comprehensive in style, covering a wide range of perils including liability insurance.

Policy administration

Apart from small craft policies which are written and issued by many companies, all marine policies are written on a standard policy form at Lloyd's or by companies. These policies detail the assured, the amounts and property covered. Details of the perils, exclusions and conditions are contained in various clauses attached to the policy rather than in the printed policy itself.

Marine liabilities

The custom has been to provide insurance for three-quarters of the shipowner's liability for collisions at sea under the marine policy. The remaining quarter and all other forms of liability are catered for by associations set up for the purpose by shipowners, known as Protecting and Indemnity Clubs or P and I clubs. These clubs are discussed further in Chapter Five.

Aviation insurance

Aviation insurance is highly specialised and with the increasing size of planes, their values and potential liabilities, it is also very complex. Policies are available from Lloyd's and companies in respect of damage to aircraft, cargo, liability to passengers and others. There have been many major air disasters in recent years which, apart from the extraordinary level of claims, also result in many hundreds of deaths.

ACCIDENT AND HEALTH

During the industrial revolution a predominantly agricultural people had to learn to live with the then new machinery of the day. The early railway locomotives thundering across the countryside must have epitomised both the opportunities and the perils of the new era.

Historical perspective

These early trains were not very safe and in addition to the fire risk caused by flying sparks there was also a high probability of accidents. In 1848 the Railway Passengers Assurance Company began offering policies aimed at providing compensation in the event of an accident. The idea of personal accident insurance grew and two years later in 1850 the Accidental Death Indemnity Company issued policies providing benefit for death from any cause for a premium of £1 for every

£1,000 insured. This company went a stage further and introduced compensation for non-fatal accidents as well as cover for medical charges during any period of disability.

The next major development came when, in 1885, the Edinburgh-based company, Sickness and Accident Insurance Association, started issuing policies that provided for compensation payments in the event of all accidents and sickness. The market later limited cover to accident and certain specified diseases.

Personal accident insurance

The intention of the basic policy is to provide compensation in the event of an accident causing death or injury. What are termed "capital sums" are paid in the event of death or certain specified injuries such as the loss of limbs or eyes.

In addition to the purchase of personal accident insurance by individuals it is also possible for companies to arrange cover on behalf of their employees and many organisations arrange "group schemes" to this end.

Sickness insurance

As we saw, the early personal accident insurers saw a market for a policy that provided a weekly benefit to the insured in the event of sickness as well as accident.

Although it may still be possible to purchase a policy for personal accident and specified diseases the most common policy is now one that embraces what we have said above about personal accident cover and at the same time provides benefits in the event of disablement due to any sickness.

Permanent health

One serious drawback to this form of cover is that once a person contracts an illness or disease the insurer is unlikely to renew the policy once the twelve-month insurance year has expired. To overcome this problem a form of "permanent" cover was developed—now commonly referred to as permanent health insurance. The prospective insured is medically examined and if found suitable a policy is issued which continues in force until a specified age, normally at retirement.

LIFE ASSURANCE

Historical perspective

In the ancient worlds of Greece and Rome men came together in associations or funeral clubs to make contributions out of which burial costs would be met. Activities similar to this continued but it was in

1583 that we have the first evidence, in Britain, of life assurance as we know it today.

A policy was taken out on 18th June 1583 on the life of William Gibbons for the sum of £382.6s.8d. The contract was for twelve months and the money was to be paid if Gibbons died within the year. He did, in fact, die on 8th May 1584 and, after a slight dispute over whether twelve months meant twelve times 28 days or twelve calendar months, the money was paid. The short-term form of policy taken out by William Gibbons was typical of the type of assurance issued in these early years. The provision of life assurance continued almost unaltered for the next century with the short-term form of policy mentioned above, and a form of mutual association, similar in design to the ancient burial societies, where members contributed to a common fund out of which payments were made on the death of members.

Mutual associations

One such mutual association that grew in prosperity was the Amicable Society for a Perpetual Assurance Office founded in 1705 by Royal charter. The significance of the charter will become clear in Chapter Five when we examine the formation of insurance companies. The "Amicable" transacted business on traditional lines but in 1757 they took the daring step of guaranteeing a minimum sum to be payable in the event of death. This seemed to satisfy a demand as the company did not suffer by its boldness.

Actuarial principles

Around the turn of the century, at roughly the same time as the "Amicable" was founded, mathematicians were working on what have become known as mortality tables. Two of the most important contributions were made by Edmund Halley, the astronomer after whom Halley's comet is named, in 1693, and James Dodson, then mathematics master at the school attached to Christ's Hospital, in 1755. The intention of the mortality tables was, in part, to be able to state in mathematical terms the likelihood of persons of a given age dying. The objective they aimed at is well described by Halley when he wrote ". . . that the price of insurance on lives might be regulated by the age of the persons on whose life the insurance is made". Dodson followed this ideal and on being refused assurance by the Amicable on account of his age, ". . . determined to form a new society on a plan of assurance on more equitable terms than those of the Amicable, which takes the same premium for all ages."

He did not have to wait long. In 1762 the Equitable Life Assurance Society was formed and transacted business on the basis suggested by him. They were able to offer life assurance on level premiums that were dependent upon the age of the person when he took out the policy. This was a significant difference from previous companies. In addition they offered a whole life policy that paid the sum assured on the death of the assured persons. This was possible as the work of Dodson and others had introduced an element of science into the business of knowing how much to charge. This science is now known as actuarial science.

Life Assurance Act 1774

The next landmark in the development was the passing of the Life Assurance Act 1774, the title of which explains its purpose, "an Act for regulating insurances upon lives and prohibiting all such insurances except in cases where persons insuring shall have an interest on the life or death of the person insured".

By the end of the eighteenth century several proprietary companies (*see* Chapter Five) had been formed where policyholders did not share in profits—as they had with mutual associations. These proprietary companies were spearheaded by the Westminster Society (1792) and the Pelican Life Office (1797).

Industrial life assurance

What we have described so far has been the development of what is now known as "ordinary" life assurance. This is to be contrasted with "industrial" life assurance. The changing structure of society brought about by the industrial revolution produced the beginnings of the "industrial" classes. The men and women who worked in the new industries were not financially protected against infirmity and the onset of old age as employees are today and in order to avoid the stigma of the poor laws many friendly societies were formed. These societies, thousands of which were in existence before the end of the eighteenth century, provided some provision for sickness and funeral expenses. Out of the friendly society grew the concept of industrial life assurance with companies transacting life assurance that was especially suited to the needs and pockets of the "industrial" classes.

Ordinary life assurance

From past statistics we can tell that at the end of 1982 there were life and pensions insurance contracts in force that produced yearly premiums of £5,720 million. This gives an indication of the magnitude of the ordinary life assurance market.

What we will do now is look at the various forms of ordinary assurance and some special features that apply to life assurance.

Term assurances

This is the simplest and oldest form of assurance and provides for payment of the sum assured on death, provided death occurs within a specified term. Should the life assured survive to the end of the term then the cover ceases and no money is payable. Depending on the age of the assured this is a very cheap form of cover and suitable, for example, in the case of a young married man with medium to low income who wants to provide a reasonable sum for his wife in the event of his death. It can also be used for a variety of specific purposes such as business journeys.

Modifications in the basic form of term assurance are found in (a) convertible term and (b) decreasing term. The disadvantage of the term assurance is, of course, that premiums can be paid for some years with no benefit accruing to the assured at the end of the term. The convertible term policy gives the assured the option to convert the term policy to a whole life or endowment, both of which are described below. The decreasing term is usually effected in connection with a loan where the outstanding amount is decreasing with each payment.

Whole life assurances
The sum assured is payable on the death of the assured whenever it occurs. Premiums are payable throughout the life of the assured or, more normally, until retirement of the assured at sixty or sixty-five. Although premiums may cease at, say, age sixty the policy is still in force and should the person die at age seventy-five the policy would provide the benefits for his representatives.

Endowment assurances
Here, the sum assured is payable on a given date say, fifteen, twenty or twenty-five years ahead. Should the policyholder live until the "maturity" date, whenever it may be, the policy will pay the sum assured. In addition the sum assured is payable on death prior to the maturity date. This type of policy is expensive, as the sum assured will be paid out for certain, but the longer the term and the earlier in life a person starts such a policy the better.

Endowment assurance is very popular with those buying houses. The assurance policy is taken out for the amount of the loan, or mortgage if a building society is involved, and written in such a way that the sum assured is payable to the lender or Society. The borrower then pays the interest and the premium. At the end of the term of the loan the endowment policy matures and repays the amount borrowed, the capital sum, to the lender, In the unlooked for event of the borrower dying prior to the end of the repayment period the endowment policy will mature and repay the capital sum.

This can be an expensive method of protecting a loan for house purchase and many building societies are now prepared to accept a modification involving a decreasing term and endowment combination that is considerably less expensive but still provides the same security.

Family income benefits

One area of financial hardship identified by those developing life assurance policies was that caused by the death of the breadwinner of a family during the time his family were growing up. A family income policy, called different names by different assurers, is a combination of whole life or endowment and decreasing term. On the death of the life assured it pays a capital sum and an income for the remainder of the policy term.

Children

Many people wish to make special arrangements for their children and two common schemes are the child's deferred assurance and the school fees policy.

Under a child's deferred assurance a policy is effected on the life of a parent with an "option" date normally coinciding with the child's eighteenth or twenty-first birthday. Should the parent survive till the option date the child has the option of continuing the policy in his own name from then on as either an endowment or whole life. The policy can be continued without further medical examination and this can be extremely important where a child has contracted an illness which would otherwise make effecting a policy difficult or extremely expensive. A lump sum can also be taken at the option date rather than an election to continue cover. In the event of the parent dying before the option date the policy is continued, without payment of premiums, until the option date. Should the child die before the stated age the premium can be returned to the parent or the policy continued.

Provision for school fees can be made by effecting an endowment policy, on the life of the parent, payable in instalments over the period of schooling.

Annuities

Certain of the assurances mentioned above have had the aim of ensuring an income of one form or another. An annuity is a method by which a person can receive a yearly sum, an annuity, in return for the payment to an insurance company of a sum of money. This is not life assurance as we have described it but it is dealt with by life assurance companies and is based on actuarial principles.

When a person has a reasonably large sum of money and wants to provide an income for himself after he retires or at some other time he could approach a life assurance company and purchase an annuity. The annuity may start at once (an immediate annuity), or may start at some date in the future (a deferred annuity). Regardless of when it starts it can take various forms. It may provide an annuity for the life of the person, the annuitant, or it may be payable irrespective of death for a certain period as in the case of the annuity certain. The guaranteed annuity is similar in that it provides the annuity for a guaranteed period or until the annuitant dies. The reversionary annuity provides for payment to the annuitant, say the wife, on the death of another named person, say the husband. The joint and survivor annuity is payable while two people, husband and wife, are alive and on the death of one will continue at the same or smaller rate on the life of the survivor.

Special features of life assurance

The provision of life assurance is a quite different process from the provision of non-life insurance. The main distinction is that in life assurance the event being assured is certain to happen in the case of those policies paying on death, or is scientifically calculable in the event of policies not paying a benefit on death.

Premium payments

As we saw under "Actuarial principles" above, premiums are payable by level amounts throughout the period of the policy. This means that each person pays the same amount throughout, that amount being determined by his age on effecting the policy. Premiums can be paid annually, half-yearly, quarterly or monthly and are often met by standing orders with banks whereby the policyholder instructs his bank to make the appropriate payments at the right times.

Participation in profits

Life assurance companies value their assets and liabilities at regular intervals, some every year and others every three years. This valuation of their operation allows them to determine if any surplus exists after calculating all future liabilities and other contingencies. Should such a surplus exist it is distributed among those policyholders who have "with profits" or "participating" policies.

Surrender values

When a person no longer wishes to continue his policy or for some reason cannot continue the premiums he can ask for the surrender value. He ceases payment and receives, not a proportion of the sum assured, but a proportion of the premiums. Not all policies allow a surrender value but where one is possible it may be less than the aggregate amount of all premiums paid, unless the policy has been in force for many years, when the surrender value may be more than the premiums paid.

Paid-up policies

An alternative to the surrender value with some policies is the paid-up policy. In this case the premiums cease; the policy continues but on maturity a smaller sum than would originally have been paid will be due to the policyholder. Depending on the policy and the company concerned these paid-up policies may or may not continue to participate in profits.

Tax relief

When the policyholder is paying income tax he may be entitled to income tax relief on the life assurance premiums if the policy was taken out before March 1984. Relief is granted provided:

(a) the policy qualifies for tax relief; the rules for qualification are fairly complex but the majority of policies were eligible;

(b) the policy is on the life of the income tax payer or that of his or her spouse; and

(c) the premiums are paid by the income tax payer or his/her spouse.

Prior to 6th April 1979 a person paid the full, gross, premium and subsequently received the appropriate tax relief in the form of an allowance included in his tax coding. Following the Finance Act 1976 the system changed from 6th April 1979 and now each person pays the net premium, after tax relief, to the insurance company and the company claims the balance, representing the tax relief, from the Inland Revenue. The rate of relief is 15 per cent of gross premium payable subject to premiums not exceeding £1,500 or one-sixth of income, whichever is the higher. Those who not taxpayers benefit from this system as everyone, regardless of whether they pay income tax or not, enjoys the benefit of the relief.

Since March 1984 this relief is no longer allowable on new contracts.

Investments

We have already identified the life assurance industry as being of considerable size. This was evidenced by the number of policies in force and the value of premiums paid each year. These vast amounts of money are held by companies to meet future liabilities and, are termed long-term funds. The total value of such funds for long-term assurance in 1982 was some £82,047 million.

These funds do not lie dormant waiting on claims coming in. They are invested to provide income for the companies and so assist policyholders and shareholders. Not only do these two groups benefit but the country as a whole benefits as the funds are invested in many forms that encourage expansion of industry and promote job employment. A look around any town or city will show how many new building projects are being sponsored by life assurance companies.

Industrial life assurance

There are very many more industrial life assurance policies in force than ordinary life policies but they are for smaller amounts. The policies in force at the end of 1982 produced yearly premiums of £1,019 million. It will thus be seen that, while there were nearly four times as many industrial policies as there were ordinary policies, they produced less than one-fifth of the premiums paid. There are some 58 collecting friendly societies and 12 authorised companies transacting industrial life assurance. Eleven of those companies account for about 98 per cent of all business done.

Endowment and whole life assurances are the most popular forms of contracts in the industrial assurance sector, normally with low sums assured. It is also common to see recurring endowments which provide whole life cover and the payment of small amounts at regular intervals, say each five years.

Pensions

There are over ten million people in pension and life assurance schemes in Britain. These schemes provide a variety of benefits for members but the main aim is to ensure that some form of pension is available on retirement.

Since April 1978 the state pension scheme consists of two parts, a basic flat-rate pension and an additional earnings related pension up to a ceiling in earnings. This scheme operates in conjunction with other pension schemes and employers can "contract out" of the additional pension part of the state scheme, by providing at least as good benefits under some private arrangement.

SELF-ASSESSMENT QUESTIONS

Select the correct option or options under each of the questions shown below.

1. (a) Fire insurance originated during the industrial revolution.
   (b) A standard policy is used for almost all business insurances.
   (c) The Theft Act 1968 made theft insurance compulsory.
   (d) An "all risks" policy has certain risks excluded.
2. (a) Employers' liability insurance is compulsory.

(b) The employers' liability policy relates to the employer's legal liability to pay damages to injured employees.

(c) Private individuals have no need of public liability insurance.

(d) Public liability insurance had its origin in boiler explosions.

3. Some forms of marine insurance policy available are:

(a) a voyage policy operative for a fixed period usually not exceeding twelve months;

(b) a mixed policy covering the subject matter for the voyage and a period of time thereafter;

(c) building risk policy for warehouse buildings;

(d) floating policy for cargo where a large initial sum assured is reduced by subsequent shipments.

CHAPTER THREE

The Functions of Insurance

CHAPTER OBJECTIVES

After studying this chapter you should be able to:
* identify the primary function of insurance as a risk transfer mechanism;
* identify the main methods by which insurers contribute to the reduction of losses;
* assess the role of insurers as institutional investors;
* assess the contribution made by insurers and brokers to invisible exports.

PRIMARY FUNCTIONS

The principal function of insurance is often expressed as spreading the losses of the few over the many. It is a means whereby the unfortunate persons suffering loss can be indemnified (*see* Chapter Nine) or compensated from the contributions of others exposed to the risk of similar losses. As the numbers of persons suffering a certain type of loss will be relatively few compared with the numbers at risk to that category of loss, the contribution falling on any one individual or firm should be relatively light.

The level of compensation is either agreed when the contract is arranged, as in life and personal accident policies, or is a direct measure of the insured's loss, subject to the terms and conditions of the policy, as in fire, marine or motor policies.

Risk transfer

Insurance is a risk transfer mechanism, whereby the individual or the business enterprise can shift some of the uncertainty of life on to the shoulders of others. In return for a known premium, usually a very small amount compared with the potential loss, the cost of that loss can be transferred to an insurer. Without insurance, there would a great deal of uncertainty experienced by an individual or an enterprise, not only as to whether a loss would occur, but also as to what size it would be if it did occur.

For example, a houseowner will realise that each year several hundred houses are damaged by fire. His uncertainty is whether in the coming year his house will be one of those damaged, and he is also uncertain whether, given that he will be one of the unlucky ones, his loss will amount to a hundred pounds or so for the redecoration of his kitchen or whether the house will be gutted and cost him thousands of pounds to repair. Even although the probability of his house becoming one of the loss statistics is extremely low, the average houseowner will nevertheless elect to spend, say £25 to £30 on house insurance, rather than face the extremely remote possibility of losing a house worth £20,000.

In the case of business enterprises, the values exposed to loss are usually much higher, but in addition the hazards inherent in their operations are often higher than those of the houseowner, and so the premium charged is likely to be substantially higher than that for a house. Even in these circumstances the majority of firms prefer to pay a known cost or premium for the transfer of risk, rather than face the uncertainty of carrying the risk of loss.

The common pool

In the previous chapter it was seen that in the early days of marine insurance, the merchants agreed to make contributions to those suffering loss after the loss had taken place. This practice did not fully transfer the cost of uncertainty, it merely reduced it. A merchant undertaking a voyage would have the risk of a total loss removed from him, but the exact amount of his share of a loss could not be determined until after the event had taken place.

This state of affairs is not ideal and modern insurance practice fixes the insured's contributions (the premium) at the inception of the contract, so that he knows the full extent of his required share of losses for that year. It may, of course, vary in the light of the claims' costs for future years.

The insured's premium is received by the insurer into a fund or pool for that type of risk, and the claims of those suffering losses are paid out of this pool. An insurance company will pay its motor claims out of the monies it has received from those insuring motor cars, and so on. Because of the large number of clients in any particular fund or pool the insurance company can predict, with reasonable accuracy, the amount of claims likely to be incurred in the coming year. There will be some variation in claims costs from year to year and the premiums include a small margin to build up a reserve upon which the company can draw in bad years. Therefore, subject to the limitations of the type of cover bought, the insured will not be required to make further contributions to the common pool after the loss.

Equitable contributions or premiums

Assuming that a risk mechanism has been set up through a common fund or pool, the third primary function is that the contributions paid into the fund should be fair to all the parties participating.

Each party wishing to insure will bring to the fund differing degrees of risk of loss to the fund. For example, a timber-built house presents a different hazard from that of one of standard brick construction; an 18-year-old driver is more hazardous than one aged 35; two 35-year-old drivers, one with a family saloon and one with a high-powered sports car, present different hazards; someone grossly overweight has a higher chance of early death than a person of average weight; a factory worker is likely to have a higher chance of injury than a office worker; the man with a house worth £50,000 has a potentially larger claim on the fund than one with a house worth £25,000.

These examples could be summarised under two main headings, hazard and value, and in aggregate the contributions to the fund must be sufficient to meet the total cost of claims brought about by these factors. In addition, there will be the costs of administering the fund, of creating reserves to ensure that abnormally heavy claims in future years can still be met, and an allowance for a margin of profit to the insurers in their operations.

Factors such as these must be taken into account by the underwriter, i.e. the person accepting the proposal on behalf of the insurers. In fixing the level of premium for each case he must try to ensure that the level of contribution made to the fund by a particular policyholder is equitable compared with the contributions of others, bearing in mind the likely frequency and severity of claims which may be made by that policyholder. Finally the level of premium fixed must be relatively competitive otherwise the insurer will go out of business due to lack of new orders.

To summarise the primary function of insurance is to provide a risk transfer mechanism by means of a common pool into which each policyholder pays a fair and equitable premium, according to the risk of loss he or she brings to the pool.

SUBSIDIARY FUNCTIONS

Stimulus to business enterprise

The main stimulus to enterprise is the release of funds, now available for investment in the productive side of a business, which would otherwise need to be held in easily accessible reserves if the firm had not transferred the risk to an insurer. Medium and large sized firms would probably create reserve funds for emergencies which might put their whole future viability in jeopardy. While these funds could be invested it would be imprudent to invest any sizeable part of them in the business and the rate of return which could be obtained externally for quickly realisable investments would be less than if the money were available for internal investment. The premium payable to an insurer, however, would only be a small proportion of the fund required because of the pooling arrangements, and so most of this money could be invested in new plant, buildings or stock.

Security

In the small firm, the security from loss which insurance provides means that losses which would be crippling can now be faced with confidence. Even in the larger firm, the executives can concentrate on their proper function of running an efficient enterprise. They can concentrate on the production and trading risks without the worry that the objectives in these fields may not be achieved due to fire or other insurable risk.

A healthy and vigorous economy usually has available to it a well-organised insurance market. The American writers Mehr and Cammack observe (*Principles of Insurance,* 1972) that the rise of Britain as a great trading nation and the fact that the country had exceptionally sound fire insurance facilities at the same period was no coincidence. Several writers are of the opinion that insurance helps to bring about a closer approach to an optimum allocation of the factors of production and hence optimum price levels. Frequently those wishing to invest in new projects will only do so if the maintainance of adequate insurance cover is written into the construction contract.

International trade is stimulated also. A marine cargo policy is one of the essential documents which, along with a letter of credit, bill of lading, bill of exchange and export invoice, enable the seller of goods to ask his bank to discount the bill of exchange and so obtain funds immediately. This avoids the necessity of having funds tied up in cargo on the high seas.

Loss prevention

When risks, apart from the very smallest, are proposed to an insurance company, they will carry out a survey in order to assess the degree of risk and therefore the acceptability of the proposal. Fire surveyors are trained to identify sources of potential risk in the production process, storage of materials, use of electricity, and so on. They make recommendations which will limit the incidence of loss from these sources.

Theft surveyors make recommendations for the protection of property against thieves. The protective devices installed on their recommendation will deter many casual thieves, again reducing the number of losses.

In a similar manner, the liability surveyor will endeavour to advise the businessman or employer in ways to prevent claims from the public, due to their operations or products, or from employees due to unsafe conditions of work.

Ideally, these experts should be consulted at the planning stage of a project, but as yet too few architects and planners realise the valuable help which is available to them and their clients. The recommendations will probably require to be incorporated into the building or plant at a later date in any event, and it is much less costly to have the loss-prevention measures incorporated at the building stage. Pressure and lifting plant and ships are required by statute to be inspected by competent engineers and these people are often employed by insurance companies. These types of plant are usually inspected during construction and again at frequent intervals during their lifetime.

Research and liaison
Insurers actively contribute to research into the prevention of loss and liaise with various public and private bodies in this connection. Details of the insurers' organisations such as FIRTO, FOC and BIA are discussed in detail in Chapter Five.

Loss control
The various surveyors mentioned above are concerned not only with preventing loss (which can never be achieved fully due to human limitations), but also with the limitation or control of any losses which do occur. For example, the Fire Offices' Committee lays down rules and regulations as to the construction of buildings, design of fire doors, sprinkler installations, and alarm systems, so that fires which do start may be contained for sufficient time to enable the public fire service to get to the scene and extinguish the blaze before it becomes a major disaster.

Similarly the theft surveyor is aware that he cannot prevent the determined criminal from entering a building, but he can make it a difficult, time-consuming and noisy process so that the quantity of material stolen may be limited.

Salvage corps
Until March 1984 the insurers maintained salvage corps in Glasgow, Liverpool and London. It was the job of the salvage corps to attend serious fires and attempt to reduce the losses which flow from things like water damage, smoke damage and pilferage. Often these costs could be substantial and the corps must have saved large amounts of money over the years.

Loss adjusters
The investigation of losses, their causes and the values involved, is often a highly technical process which requires very quick action after the loss in order to assess these factors accurately and to take steps to minimise further loss.

It would be uneconomic for insurers to have teams of experts in various fields scattered around the country, as many of them would be under-employed for much of the time. This problem has been overcome by independent firms of loss adjusters setting up offices in the larger towns and cities, and providing these services on a fee basis to the insurers in the locality. These experts contribute greatly to the limitation of the cost of loss, by knowing how best to get a business on its feet again quickly, where to purchase or hire temporary plant, where to dispose of salvage at the best price, and so on.

Social benefits

The benefits to society are much wider than the estimated amounts for destruction of buildings and contents by fire (£565.6 million in 1983) or crime claims (£235.3 million in 1982).

The fact that a factory owner has adequate fire insurance cover means that he has the capital to reinstate his factory and so recreate jobs for his workers, who might otherwise be unemployed for a considerable time. Frequently several firms in an area are dependent on other firms, either as customers or as suppliers, and so they too may be at risk. When the multiplier effect of the reduced income of a group of workers is taken into account society at large in that locality may suffer if a firm goes into liquidation after an uninsured loss. If full consequential loss (loss of profits) insurance has been arranged in addition to the material loss cover, there may not be the need for even temporary lay-offs of workers following a major loss.

The aid which insurance provides in maintaining industry in an area stabilises the economy of that area and in aggregate helps to stabilise the national economy through the continued sources of rates and taxes.

Although most developed countries enjoy to some extent the benefits of comprehensive welfare payments from the state, these are sometimes limited in amount (e.g. death benefits, widows' and old age pensions). However, the individual can purchase, through life assurance, income benefits and lump sums for dependants and many employers provide group life assurance, pension benefits and disablement schemes for their employees, thus supplementing the state benefits. Without these benefits being available from the insurance market, the state benefits would require to be increased for a much wider range of people than at present. Failing this, many more of our sick, aged and bereaved would be impoverished.

Savings

Another benefit which stems from the provision of life assurance cover is the use of endowment assurances as a means of saving. The most frequent users of these contracts wish to save a lump sum for retirement, or take out a policy in conjunction with a house purchase mortgage or for children's education or majority. These contracts are long-term ones, and the temptation to end the contract early has financial penalties by way of surrender values below the value paid in. The saver is therefore more inclined to keep on paying the premium compared with saving in a bank or building society. Life assurance premiums, subject to certain rules, used to enjoy tax relief: this advantage was abolished in the Finance Act 1984.

ASSOCIATED FUNCTIONS

When a risk transfer system is set up there are certain functions which evolve from those operations which are not the direct result of the desire to transfer risk or obtain benefits for society. Insurers, as custodians of the premiums paid, invest these funds so that they are available when required. This may be within the next twelve months in the case of property claims, the next two or three years in the case of liability claims, or in anything up to forty or fifty years in the case of life assurance. Since London is the main insurance centre of the world the transactions of British insurers extend throughout the world, and when they are carrying foreign risks there is a flow of overseas earnings, or as they are often called "invisible exports", into Britain to help the balance of payments.

Investments of funds

As indicated above, when an insurance premium is received into the fund, any likely claims will arise some time in the future, from a few weeks or months until several years. The insurers must try to obtain the best overall return on the investment of these funds. This will usually be a mixture of high interest rates and the highest capital appreciation in order to keep pace with inflation and to increase profits.

A wide spread of different types of investment is desirable for safety reasons, and by making this spread of investments the insurance market helps national and local governments in their short and medium term borrowings, industry and commerce by loans of various kinds and in providing working capital by taking up share issues. Life and pension funds may be invested in property owned by the insurers or in which they have a major interest and leased to various commercial interests. This latter type of investment has proved to be excellent for capital appreciation over the years and provides an income each year by way of rents. A summary of these investments is given opposite for 1982.

	Long-term funds (£m)	General funds (£m)
British Government Authority securities	21,681	3,777
Foreign and Commonwealth Government provincial and municipal stocks	2,739	3,709
Debentures, loan stocks preference and guaranteed stocks and shares	3,734	2,957
Ordinary stocks and shares	28,065	5,100
Mortgages	5,100	742
Real property and ground rents	17,267	2,041
Other investments	3,461	1,757
	82,047	20,083

This produces a total investment of £102,130,000,000. (Source: *BIA Members Statistics* 1982)

Invisible earnings or invisible exports

In earlier discussions it was shown how individuals and firms seek to transfer risks to insurers. It is sometimes necessary in the case of very severe risks or very large risks to spread these insurances around the market so that any loss will not fall too severely on any one company. On occasions it is necessary to go beyond national boundaries either because of the size of the risk to be insured or because of a lack of market facilities in a particular type of insurance in a particular country.

Over the last few hundreds of years the British market, centred on London, has been able to provide the greatest security and the widest range of cover. From Fig. 2 it can be seen that "insurance" contributed £1,174 million towards our invisible earnings. This represented 27 per cent of the invisible earnings of all financial institutions in 1982.

Prior to the advent of North Sea oil it was usually these *invisible earnings* which compensated for the continual deficit in the balance of trade in *visible* goods.

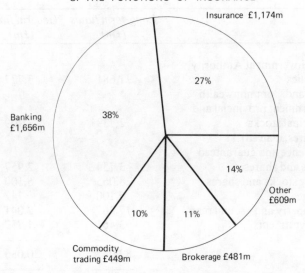

[Source: *Insurance Facts and Figures*, BIA, 1982]
Fig. 2. *Net invisible earnings of UK financial institutions (1982).*

SELF-ASSESSMENT QUESTIONS

Select the correct options in each of the following statements.

1. The primary function of insurance is:
   (*a*) to control the incidence and severity of losses;
   (*b*) to create investment funds for industry;
   (*c*) to transfer the risk of loss to others;
   (*d*) to earn profits for the shareholders of the insurance companies.
2. Insurers contribute to the reduction of losses by:
   (*a*) employing surveyors to inspect premises and make recommendations for improvement;
   (*b*) supplying security teams to guard premises;
   (*c*) carrying out research into losses and their causes;
   (*d*) maintaining fire brigades in certain cities.
3. Insurers must invest all their funds in:
   (*a*) short term high yield securities;
   (*b*) a mixture of short and long term investments;
   (*c*) mortgages;
   (*d*) government stocks.
4. (*a*) The insurance market is the largest single source of "invisible" earnings from overseas.

(b) The insurance market is the second largest source of "invisible" overseas earnings.

(c) British insurance earnings from overseas are less than are spent overseas in premiums.

(d) The balance of payments figure is part of the balance of trade figure.

CHAPTER FOUR

Government Supervision

CHAPTER OBJECTIVES

After studying this chapter you should be able to:
* outline the historical background to government supervision of insurance.
* assess the extent to which government supervision is necessary in the public interest;
* outline the provisions relating to compulsory insurance in relevant statutes;
* recognise and apply the main provisions of current legislation relating to the supervision of insurance;
* outline the provisions of EEC Directives which have a bearing on the conduct of insurance in the United Kingdom or within the EEC.

ROLE OF GOVERNMENT SUPERVISION

Historical development of government supervision

Government has always taken an interest in insurance activities and it is interesting to speculate why this should have been. Before going on to suggest reasons why there should be some element of state control we will look back and trace the growth of this supervision.

Possibly the earliest record of government intervention in Britain was the Chamber of Assurances founded in 1575 (*see* Chapter Two), whereby marine policies had to be registered. The pattern of "modern" supervision, however, could be said to have started in 1870 with the Life Assurance Companies Act.

Life Assurance Companies Act 1870. This Act made it obligatory for life assurance companies to make a deposit of £20,000 with the High Court before they could transact business. In addition detailed accounting and actuarial returns had to be made to the Board of Trade in order that the solvency, the extent to which assets exceeded liabilities, could be monitored. Similar controls were also imposed on companies transacting employers' liability insurance by the Employers' Liability Insurance Companies Act 1907.

Assurance Companies Act 1909. By this Act the supervision of insurance business was extended beyond life assurance to fire, personal accident and bond investment. Lloyd's underwriters were exempted from the provisions of the Act provided they complied with specified requirements. This Act was the framework upon which supervision of insurance was built for more than half a century.

Industrial Assurance Act 1923. This Act provided that industrial assurance was to be treated as a separate class of business (it has since been incorporated in later legislation), and limited its transaction to certain specified organisations. One major innovation was the establishment of an Industrial Assurance Commissioner who was to exercise the statutory powers of the Department of Trade and Industry in relation to Industrial Life Assurance.

Assurance Companies Act 1946. Since the passing of the 1909 Act several new classes of business had been introduced and their regulation was incorporated in this 1946 Act. Motor, aviation and transit insurances were brought within the scope of the Act as was the more established marine business. The main reason for noting this Act is, however, the fact that it abolished the need for deposits and replaced them with a new system. Several insurance companies had found their liabilities exceeding their assets, the amount they had to pay or were to pay in the future exceeding the amount of money they had to meet these payments. In the main this was attributable to the substantial growth in motor insurance business; not all companies who offered insurance were in a financially sound position so to do. The Assurance Companies (Winding Up) Acts 1933 to 1935 are evidence of the need for some tightening up of insurers' financial reserves.

Solvency margins. In place of the deposits, in the case of non-life business, companies were required to satisfy certain solvency requirements measured in terms of solvency margins. The margin related to the amount by which assets were to exceed liabilities. In brief this meant that each company had to maintain a balance between how much it had in terms of assets and how much it knew it had to pay or would be likely to pay in liabilities. The exact requirement under the 1946 Act was that each company should have (*a*) a minimum paid-up share capital of £50,000 and (*b*) assets exceeding liabilities by £50,000 or 10 per cent of the previous year's premium income, whichever was the greater.

Insurance Companies Act 1958. The 1958 Act consolidated all the previous relevant statutes since 1909. The Act introduced certain requirements relating to accounts and audits but it is not necessary to consider it in detail.

Companies Act 1967. Part II of the Companies Act 1967 met the need for stronger power that had arisen during the early 1960s. A number of motor insurers had failed during this period, despite the solvency requirement, and fresh margins for non-life business were set. The new requirements were:

(a) a minimum paid-up share capital of £100,000;

(b) in the first year of trading assets must exceed liabilities by £50,000;

(c) in subsequent trading periods assets were to exceed liabilities by £50,000 where the premium income in the previous year was not greater than £250,000, but where the premium income exceeded £250,000 the margin was to be at least 20 per cent on the first £2,500,000 plus 10 per cent on the balance of that income.

Regulations relating to authorisation of insurers, reinsurance requirements, management of companies, initial conduct of business, actuarial valuation of life funds and insolvency and winding up were also made. Following the collapse of the Vehicle and General Insurance Company in 1971, and the report of the Scott Committee on Property Bonds and Equity Linked Life Assurance in 1973, came the Insurance Companies Amendment Act 1973 which introduced additional regulatory powers.

Other statutes

In 1974 the Insurance Companies Act consolidated the 1958, 1967 and 1973 provisions in one statute and one year later the Policyholders Protection Act 1975 provided a means by which policyholders could be compensated when insurers became insolvent. In 1977 the Insurance Brokers (Registration) Act introduced the Insurance Brokers Registration Council to consider the registration of brokers according to their qualifications and experience. The title of the Act sets forth its object, "an Act to provide for the registration of insurance brokers and for the regulation of their professional standards, and for purposes connected therewith".

These Acts are all evidence of the strength of feeling that insurance was an activity requiring some measure of supervision and regulation. The current piece of legislation relating to companies themselves is the Insurance Companies Act 1982 of which more is said later.

Why have state regulation?

Having looked at the historical development of governmental intervention in insurance activities we can suggest some reasons why such supervision is necessary. The words control, regulation, supervision and intervention are being looked upon as interchangeable although some have attached separate meanings to each. For our purposes we can say that governments have taken more than a passing interest in the transaction of insurance and whether we say this interest amounted to intervention, control, regulation or supervision is incidental to the question "why have state legislation?" The main justification for state control is to protect the public, but this aim is also accompanied by one relating to socially desirable measures. In the following six paragraphs the first three relate to protection and the second three to social measures.

Maintain solvency. Perhaps the greatest step taken by legislation was to introduce solvency margins that were related to premium income. In this way a ratio was established between the margin and the amount of business undertaken. This prevented certain people with fraudulent aims from providing insurance and acted as a continual monitor on those already transacting it.

Equity. The term "equity" has been used but equally suitable would have been morality, fairness or reasonableness, as each imply the fact that an element of fairness must exist between companies and policyholders. The insurance contract is one of considerable complexity and it is essential that controls exist for the protection of policyholders.

Competence. The buying and selling of insurance is unlike very many other forms of product purchasing. A tangible product is not being purchased; what is being bought and sold is a promise to provide indemnity (*see* Chapter Nine). It is necessary that those who deal in such promises are competent persons and able to fulfil their pledges when the need arises. Regulations are necessary therefore in the management of insurance companies.

Insurable interest. Insurable interest is one of the basic doctrines of insurance and will be studied in some detail in Chapter Eight. Governments have found it necessary to introduce legislation to eradicate any element of gambling. Reference has already been made to this point in Chapters One and Two. It was not acceptable that unscrupulous persons should benefit by effecting policies of insurances where they had no financial interest in the potential loss other than the profit they would make if it occurred.

Provision of certain forms of insurance. An element of intervention has been in evidence where forms of cover have been made compulsory, as in the case of employers' liability and third party motor accident injuries. The intervention is not in the provision of cover, by government, but in establishing the nature of the cover to be granted.

National Insurance. For some areas of social risk the government's intervention has been total and it has assumed the responsibility for providing certain covers. A full examination of National Insurance schemes is covered in Chapter Eleven and it is sufficient to say here that for areas such as unemployment, sickness and widows benefits the state carries the risk under the national scheme.

Nationalisation

In 1976 the Labour Party accepted proposals, at its annual conference, for nationalisation of Britain's seven largest insurance companies and in

1978 the insurance industry completed its evidence to the Wilson Committee that had been set up to review the functioning of insurance institutions. As yet no companies have been nationalised but this does not mean that the issue is dead and we should certainly acquaint ourselves with the arguments for and against. The topic is one that arouses deep feelings and it is often difficult to put forward a balanced and objective portrayal of the arguments for and against. The following represent certain of the basic points on each side.

For nationalisation

(a) Governmental control of funds would be to the benefit of society at large.

(b) It would be possible to introduce uniformity in wordings and practice.

(c) Statistics could be pooled.

(d) Premium rates could be reduced in the absence of the profit motive.

(e) The costly exercise of making the statutory returns would be eliminated.

(f) There would not be so great a reliance on reinsurance with a commensurate saving in costs.

(g) It may be better if those forms of insurance made compulsory by government were provided by the state.

Against nationalisation

(a) It is difficult to "nationalise the international". It could be that some overseas countries would not trade with a government-owned insurance industry.

(b) Insurance has grown and developed in private hands for many centuries and there is no reason to think that any better service would result from state ownership.

(c) Experience of certain nationalised industries is one of overloaded bureaucracy.

(d) Competition encourages efficiency and innovation.

(e) The present tax revenue from insurance companies would be lost.

(f) The large-scale nature of any state insurance organisation may lead to a strictness in practice and interpretation that would not benefit the public.

(g) The government have no experience in underwriting insurance risks.

COMPULSORY INSURANCE

Motor insurance

The Road Traffic Act 1972, Part VI, consolidates previous legislation. Section 143 of the Act states that "Subject to the provisions of this Part of this Act, it shall not be lawful for a person to use, or cause or permit another person to use, a motor vehicle on a road unless there is in force in relation to the use of the vehicle by that person or that other person, as the case may be, such a policy of insurance or such a security in respect of third party risks as complies with the requirement of this Part of this Act. . . ."

In brief we can say that:

(a) The third party risks referred to are death of or bodily injury to any person. This will include pedestrians, passengers in other cars, passengers in the policyholder's car and any other person at all.

(b) The security, in place of insurance, is a deposit of £15,000 with the Accountant General of the Supreme Court and this will remove the need to insure only when the car is driven under the control of the insured.

(c) A certificate of insurance is to be issued and a policy will not be effective in the terms of the Road Traffic Act unless one is. Note that a certificate of insurance is one of the documents required before a person can obtain a Road Fund Licence.

(d) It is the user of the car, not the driver, who must be covered by insurance and a person will be deemed to have the use of a car when he retains an element of control, management or operation of the vehicle at the relevant time.

(e) The policy of insurance is to be issued by an "authorised" insurer, an insurer carrying on motor insurance in Great Britain and who has satisfied the requirement of the Insurance Companies Act 1982. Such an insurer must also be a member of the Motor Insurers' Bureau.

Employers' liability insurance

The Employers' Liability (Compulsory Insurance) Act 1969 came into effect on 1st January 1972 and from that date every employer carrying on business in Scotland, England and Wales, had to insure against liability for bodily injury or disease sustained by employees and arising from their employment. Note the following points. (Separate statutes apply to other parts of the United Kingdom.)

(a) The Act refers only to bodily injury and disease and while it therefore covers a whole range of claims it does not include any element of property damage.

(b) The policy must be effected with an "authorised" insurer and in this connection the points applying to an "authorised" motor insurer apply here also.

(c) A certificate of insurance is to be issued and must be displayed at every place of business.

(d) The person injured must be employed by the policyholder and the injury or disease must arise out of that employment.

(e) Certain employers need not insure, such as local government councils and industries under national ownership or control.

Riding establishments: public liability insurance

By the Riding Establishments Act 1970, which amended the Riding Establishments Act 1964, any person who holds a licence to run a riding establishment must have certain liability insurance. Insurance is to be held against liability for any injury sustained by a person who hires a horse or who is being instructed, and is also required for liability which may be incurred by the hirer in connection with injury caused to any other person.

Nuclear risks

Organisations holding a licence to operate a nuclear plant, in Britain usually governmental agencies, have a duty imposed upon them by the Nuclear Installations Act 1965 to ensure that no injury or damage is caused either on or off the site by nuclear perils. A further stipulation is that funds are to be made available to meet any liabilities devolving upon the operator, by way of insurance or other approved means. The amount to be made available is £5 million for each nuclear installation and is an aggregate amount, i.e. it will reduce with each claim payment. This £5 million is not the limit of funding against the nuclear peril as the government has made provision for compensation up to £43 million per occurrence.

Solicitors' professional indemnity

By the Solicitors Act 1974 it is now compulsory for every solicitor to carry professional indemnity insurance with a limit of indemnity amounting to at least £50,000, or £30,000 for each partner in a partnership.

Oil pollution

There have been several cases of oil spillage causing damage to fish stocks, wild life and pollution of coastlines. The Merchant Shipping (Oil Pollution) Act 1971 requires certain oil-carrying vessels to show a certificate proving proof of insurance.

Why have compulsory insurance?

There are one or two additional areas where insurance is required, but is not complulsory. Examples are the case of contractors who want a tax-exemption certificate from the Inland Revenue, where they would have to hold public liability insurance; a mortgagor buying a house would find that the building society insisted on building insurance. Insurance in such cases is not, strictly speaking, compulsory; why, then, are certain forms of insurance compulsory in particular cases? The following are suggested as being among the reasons:

(a) *The provision of funds.* There would be no point in awarding damages to someone if there was no money to meet the award. Notice that the insurance is for liability against injury, except in the case of nuclear sites when damage is also included, thus emphasising the importance placed upon injury in the eyes of the law. The enactment of compulsory insurance ensures, as far as possible, that funds will be available when damages are awarded. An interesting point for discussion is the extent to which this fact influences the eventual size of the award, if in fact it influences it at all.

(b) *The easement of the state's burden.* It is unlikely that the state would allow people injured at work, or in similar accidents, to go without compensation entirely and if the responsible party did not have funds to provide this the likelihood is that the state would come forward with some money. The existence of insurance eliminates this possibility.

(c) *The response to national concern.* Apart from riding establishments the areas where insurance has been made compulsory represent areas of national concern. When we traced the development of motor and employers' liability insurance we saw how public attitudes changed over the years until concern over accidents was so high that legislation was introduced to ensure the provision of insurance. Nuclear risks is a far more recent area of concern and it may be pertinent to note that it is the only risk where insurance is required for injury or damage. This may be due partly to the grave concern voiced by many and to the difficulties that could be involved in trying to separate injury and damage claims when radioactive material leaked from some installation.

(d) *Protection.* It is possible in certain instances that by making a person insure you also make him more careful, thus assisting in the protection of the potentially injured persons. This may or may not be true, but what can be said with more certainty is that as insurance is involved the insured will be exposed to all the expertise available from insurers and the exercising of this expertise may improve the risk and thus assist in protecting people. An example from the employers' liability field could be the case where a liability surveyor from an insurance company insists on special guards on machines to minimise the risk of injury. The insured may not have contemplated doing this himself but is forced to by the insurers.

CURRENT LEGISLATION GOVERNING INSURANCE TRANSACTIONS: THE INSURANCE COMPANIES ACT 1982

Since 1974, and the Insurance Companies Act of that year, there has been a large volume of legislation. This increase in legislation during the latter part of the 1970s mirrors, in part, the growth in the consumer movement in Great Britain, but may also be attributable to two other factors.

First, there were a number of insurance company failures, for example, Vehicle and General in 1971 and Nation Life in 1974. These failures may well have encouraged Parliament to take action to increase the powers which the state has in supervising the insurance business. The second factor which has promoted legislation is our membership of the European Community. Well over twenty statutory instruments were passed following the Insurance Companies Act 1974.

By the early 1980s the whole area of legislation relating to the transaction of insurance was extremely complicated. However, the Insurance Companies Act 1982, which came into effect on 28th January 1983, consolidated the position. This Act, together with certain regulations, now represents the regulatory powers of government. The implementation of the terms of the Act rest with the Insurance Division of the Department of Trade and Industry. The Act itself has one hundred sections spread over five parts, but for our purposes we can concentrate on five main areas covered by the Act.

Authorisation
Any company wishing to transact insurance must first obtain authorisation from the Department of Trade and Industry. The Department has to satisfy itself that only "fit and proper" persons should be transacting insurance. To do that the Department requires each applicant to complete a detailed questionnaire, incorporating points such as types of policies to be offered, proposed premium rates, marketing methods, estimated premium income and capital expenditure, etc.

The Department has the power in granting authorisation to require new companies not to make investments of certain forms, to restrict premium income to prescribed limits, and to make regular detailed returns about their business.

One important factor taken into account when considering an application for authorisation is the class of business the applicants intend to transact. EEC Directive 73/239/EEC introduced into British legislation seventeen classes of *general* business. These classes, together with seven *long-term* business classes, are detailed in the 1982 Act as follows:

Long-term:

  i   Life and annuity
 ii   Marriage and birth
iii   Linked long-term
 iv   Permanent health
  v   Tontines
 vi   Capital redemption
vii   Pension fund management

General:

 1 Accident
 2 Sickness
 3 Land vehicles
 4 Railway rolling stock
 5 Aircraft
 6 Ships
 7 Goods in transit
 8 Fire and natural forces
 9 Damage to property
10 Motor vehicle liability
11 Aircraft liability
12 Liability for ships
13 General liability
14 Credit
15 Suretyship
16 Miscellaneous financial loss
17 Legal expenses.

It can be seen that these classes of business relate to forms of risk rather than types of insurance business. Classes 10, 11, 12 and 13 are all forms of liability risk which would fall within liability insurance policies of one kind or another. In order that those who transact general insurance can readily identify which class relates to which type of insurance, the following table was prepared:

Designation	Composition
1 Accident and Health	Classes 1 and 2
2 Motor	Classes 3, 7, 10 and part of 1
3 Marine and transport	Classes 4, 6, 7, 12 and part of 1
4 Aviation	Classes 5, 7, 11 and part of 1
5 Fire and other damage to property	Classes 8 and 9
6 Liability	Classes 10, 11, 12 and 13
7 Credit and suretyship	Classes 14 and 15
8 General	All classes

The *tontine* mentioned in the list of long-term classes of business is now almost extinct and may not be familiar to many readers. The general idea, developed in the late seventeenth century, was for people to group together in a *tontine*. Each contributed a principal sum and received an annuity. As each member died their income was distributed among the surviving subscribers until the last member died.

Solvency

The aim of having solvency margins is to attempt to ensure that assets exceed liabilities by an agreed minimum amount. The margin cannot be expressed in absolute terms as the volume of business transacted by companies differs substantially. The margin is expressed as a ratio and the formulae by which the ratio is to be operated are detailed in the Act.

The regulations concerning the solvency margin differ depending upon whether a company is a United Kingdom company, a Community company or an external company, as follows:

United Kingdom company: one having its head office in the United Kingdom and formed under the Companies Acts, a registered society or established by Royal charter or Act of Parliament.

Community company: one having its head office in a member country of the European Community other than the United Kingdom but having a branch or agency in the UK.

External company: one with its headquarters outside the Community but with a branch or agency in the UK.

We will concentrate on United Kingdom companies. The regulations regarding solvency margins apply throughout the Community and rather than have a number of different calculations using all the different currencies the margins are expressed in European Currency Units (ECUs). The ECU is an artificial currency to which the currencies of all member states are fixed. The conversion rate for each member state is fixed by the European Commission and the rate applying on the last day of October is the one used to calculate the solvency margin for the following year. The UK conversion rate for 1984 was, for example, one ECU = 59.3782p.

Calculation of solvency margins: United Kingdom companies (General Business) The margin is determined by taking the greater of two sums resulting from the application of two sets of calculations called respectively "First Method (premium basis)" and "Second Method (claims basis)". Companies must ensure that their assets exceed their liabilities by at least the amount calculated according to the higher of the two methods.

Premium basis. Gross premiums received are transferred into ECUs at the current conversion rate. The company calculates 18 per cent of the first 10 million ECUs and 16 per cent of any balance over and above

10 million. The resultant figure is then multiplied by 50 per cent, or a higher percentage if net claims paid (claims less reinsurance recoveries) is more than 50 per cent of gross claims paid.

Example (all sums in millions)

$$\text{Gross premiums} = 15 \text{ ECU}$$
$$10 \times 18\% = 1.8$$
$$5 \times 16\% = \underline{0.8}$$
$$2.6$$

$$\text{Net claims paid} = 10$$
$$\text{Gross claims paid} = 12$$

$$\text{Solvency margin} = \frac{10}{12} \times 2.6 = \underline{2.17 \text{ ECU}}$$

Claims basis. The total of all claims paid during the preceding three years is found, converted into ECU and the average taken. Twenty-six per cent is calculated of the first 7 million ECU and 23 per cent of any excess over 7 million. The resultant figure is then multiplied by the same percentages as in the premium basis.

Example (all sums in millions)

Average claims paid 12 ECU

$$7 \times 26\% = 1.82$$
$$5 \times 23\% = \underline{1.15}$$
$$2.97$$

$$\text{Net claims paid} = 10$$
$$\text{Gross claims paid} = 12$$

$$\text{Solvency margin} = \frac{10}{12} \times 2.97 = \underline{2.48 \text{ ECU}}$$

Guarantee funds

If a community company with its head office in the UK fails to maintain a margin of solvency at least equal to the greater of (*a*) the guarantee fund, or (*b*) the minimum guarantee fund, the Secretary of State will ask the company to submit for his approval a short term financial scheme.

(*a*) *The guarantee fund* is one-third of the greater of the premium basis or the claims basis for calculating the margin of solvency.

(b) *The minimum guarantee funds* are shown below and are calculated according to the classes of business they write.

Class	Amount
10, 11, 12, 13, 14, 15	400,000 ECU
1, 2, 3, 4, 5, 6, 7, 8, 16	300,000 ECU
9, 17	200,000 ECU

The Life Establishment Directive 79/267/EEC was introduced in 1979, and one effect of its implementation was the prescribing of solvency margins for life assurance. These margins applied to new companies from 1st January 1982 and to existing assurers from 15th March 1984. When dealing with life assurance it is not simply a matter of establishing some relationship between premiums and claims. Solvency margins must rely more on actuarial valuations of potential losses and the size of fund required. Separate calculations are required for different combinations of long-term classes of business, and in the end the margin is the aggregate of these individual classes.

Monitoring

All authorised companies must deposit with the Department of Trade and Industry each year detailed accounts and other information. These returns will include revenue accounts, profit and loss accounts, balance sheets and information on claims. Where life assurance has been transacted the company must include a certificate signed by an actuary stating whether or not in his opinion the liabilities of the company's long-term business exceed the amount of those liabilities shown in the balance sheet. In addition those companies carrying on life assurance must, at least every three years, send an actuary's report on his investigation into the financial position of such long-term business.

This continual monitoring of companies, while they are transacting business, should help in identifying those companies where trouble is anticipated.

Intervention

Where the Department feel the protection of policyholders is required urgently, as in the case of a likely insolvency, or where misleading information has been supplied or a manager is not considered a fit person to run the company, and in certain other cases, it may take steps to intervene. As a result of such intervention the Department of Trade and Industry has powers to ask the company:

(a) to stop issuing or renewing policies;
(b) to stop making certain kinds of investments;
(c) to turn certain investments into cash;
(d) to maintain assets in the UK at least equal to its liabilities there.

The list of powers runs to some ten items but the above are sufficient to make the point that the Department's powers are quite substantial.

Unfortunately the existence of legislation and the granting of powers such as the above has not always resulted in the protection of the policyholder, as the collapse of Vehicle and General showed, but in other cases the legislation has proved effective.

Conduct of business

Part III of the 1982 Act is concerned with the more day-to-day management of companies as opposed to the broad financial issues discussed so far. Advertisements fall within this section of the Act. The Act says that a company must say, if it is not an *authorised* insurer, that policyholders will not be protected by the Policyholders Protection Act 1975. Another piece of information which must be provided to potential policyholders is the relationship between an insurer and an intermediary. Where an insurer owns or has a controlling interest in an insurance broking company then this must be revealed. The Vehicle and General Insurance Co., for example, owned a broker, Andrew & Booth Ltd., which produced a large volume of business for them.

Two other aspects of company activity, dealt with by this Part of the Act, are also worth mentioning. The Act makes it an offence to induce someone to effect insurance by *knowingly* making a misleading statement. It also insists that potential policyholders of long-term contracts be allowed a *cooling-off* period during which time they may decide to cancel the policy without penalty. This *cooling-off* period is to be made known by means of a cooling-off notice issued with the policy.

SELF-ASSESSMENT QUESTIONS

Attempt the following questions and then refer to the text to check your answer.

1. Why have governments showed such an interest in the regulation of insurance?
2. What are the arguments against nationalisation of the insurance industry?
3. List the forms of insurance which are now compulsory.
4. What arguments can be put forward to support the existence of compulsory insurance?

5. What is the current statute governing insurance operations?
6. What must an intending insurer do to gain authorisation to transact insurance?
7. On whom does the responsibility for supervising solvency margins rest?
8. What two methods are involved in the calculation of solvency margins?
9. How does the solvency margin relate to the guarantee fund?

CHAPTER FIVE

The Market Place

CHAPTER OBJECTIVES

After studying this chapter you should be able to:
* define, and explain the differences between, the various types of insurer;
* define, and explain the differences between and the functions of, insurance intermediaries;
* illustrate, and explain the structure of, the insurance market in the UK;
* illustrate, and explain the structure of, a typical large insurance company;
* outline the organisation of Lloyd's;
* outline the work of the various insurance organisations, e.g. the British Insurance Association, the British Insurance Brokers' Association.

GENERAL STRUCTURE OF THE MARKET PLACE

When one talks about a market place, a vision of a Saturday market in a country town, or a cattle market, or of some similar meeting place, springs to mind. Most of us have seen pictures in books, or in the media, of markets being held for the sale of grain, tobacco leaf, or stocks and shares.

In the market for insurance, however, there is no single place in the country or in a town where the buyers, sellers and middlemen meet to transact insurance. There is one exception to this general statement and that is the transaction of insurance business at Lloyd's which will be discussed in full a little later. Suffice it to say that at the moment the organisation of the Lloyd's market is unique in the world, although Lloyd's-type markets have been set up in New York and in certain other American cities.

Insurance as a service industry

Like any other market, the insurance market comprises sellers—the insurance companies and Lloyd's underwriting members; buyers—the general public, industry and commerce; and middlemen—the insurance brokers and agents (*see* Fig. 3). In other markets the buyers, sellers and perhaps the middlemen can come together to examine the merchandise which is to be the subject of the sale. With insurance, however, it is not

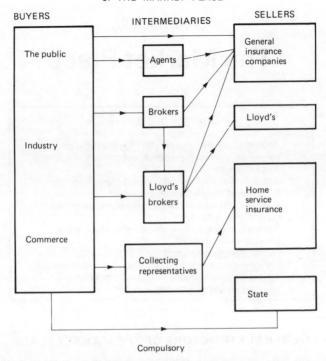

Fig. 3. *The insurance market.*

possible to bring the house, factory or ship, etc. to a market place, and in any event what is being insured is intangible; it is the financial interest in the house, factory or ship, or a potential lawsuit associated therewith, which is at risk.

Therefore, although the buying and selling of insurance takes place every hour of every working day, contracts are arranged as and when required, at a place convenient to the individual parties concerned. As was seen earlier in Chapter Three when discussing the functions of insurance, the insurance market is providing a financial service. It is a service industry in that it is supportive to industry producing goods.

This chapter discusses in detail the various parts of the insurance market, but before dealing with these aspects in depth, it may be advisable to comment briefly on some of the terms used.

The insured

The buyer of insurance, whether a private individual or a large corporation, is called the insured. It is the buyer's financial risk which is being assured by the insurer in return for a premium.

The insurer
The seller or supplier of insurance is called the insurer, and insurers can be divided into two broad classes.

Companies. These may transact one form of insurance only, e.g. life business, or they may transact many forms of cover, e.g. motor, fire, liability and perhaps life business.

Lloyd's. This is an association of individual underwriting members who form themselves into groups or syndicates but each retain their individuality.

The intermediary
A buyer of insurance (the insured) may approach a company direct, but the majority of business is placed through intermediaries. Indeed a buyer can place business at Lloyd's only through an intermediary called a Lloyd's broker. Intermediaries can be classified as follows.

Broker. An individual or firm whose full time occupation is the placing of business with insurance companies on behalf of clients.

Lloyd's broker. Similar to a broker but in addition business can be placed at Lloyd's as the firm have been approved by the committee of Lloyd's.

Agent. Someone who places insurance with companies but whose main occupation is in some field which brings him into contact with members of the public who require insurance. Examples of this class are solicitors, accountants, garage proprietors and the like.

Insurance/assurance
Reference was made in Chapter Two to the words "*in*surance" and "*as*surance". The use of either word in the title of an insurer does not give an indication of the business they transact. Hence the Royal Insurance Group and the Commercial Union Assurance Group both transact life and non-life business.

INSURERS

Proprietary companies
The majority of insurance companies come under this heading and are limited liability companies with shareholders as "proprietors".

Historically they have been created by Royal charter as in the case of the Royal Exchange Assurance; by Act of Parliament as in the case of the Scottish Union and National (now part of the Norwich Union Group); or by deed of settlement (a form of partnership). Generally, however, these companies have been reformed by registration under the Companies Acts. The majority of insurance companies have been created by registration under the Companies Acts and it is almost certain that all new companies in the future will be created in this manner.

Proprietary companies have an authorised and issued share capital to which the original shareholders subscribed, and it is to the shareholders that any profits belong after provision for expenses, reserves and, in the case of life business, with – profit policyholders' bonuses. The shareholders' liability is limited to the nominal value of their shares (hence the term "limited liability") but the company is liable for its debts and if the solvency margin cannot be met (*see* Chapter Four) the company will go into liquidation. The public can deal direct with these companies but usually an intermediary is involved. In most classes of business there is keen competition among proprietary companies and also between proprietary companies and other sectors of the market.

Mutual companies

Mutual companies have been formed by deed of settlement or registration under the Companies Acts. They are owned by the policyholders who share any profits made. The shareholder in the proprietary company receives his share of the profit by way of dividends, but in the mutual company the policyholder owner will usually enjoy lower premiums or higher life assurance bonuses than would otherwise be the case.

Originally, the policyholders could be called upon to make further contributions to the fund if the original premiums were inadequate to meet the claims and expenses. Nowadays most mutual insurers are limited by guarantee with the policyholders' maximum liability limited to their premiums or, at the most, an additional 50p or £1.

It is no longer possible to tell from the name of a company whether it is proprietary or mutual. Many companies which were originally formed as mutual organisations have now registered under the Companies Acts as proprietary companies although they have retained the word "mutual" in their title. Others, registered as companies limited by guarantee and without the word "mutual" in their title, are, in fact, owned by the policyholders.

Mutual indemnity associations

Mutual indemnity associations differ from mutual companies, in that the companies will accept business from the public at large, whereas an indemnity association originally would only accept business from members of a particular trade. Over the years many of the associations have had to accept business from members of the public in order to have greater financial stability and spread of risk and have been reformed as mutual or proprietary companies.

The true mutual indemnity associations grew out of trade associations and are common pools into which members of a particular trade contribute, and from which they can make a claim when necessary. The associations were formed because members of a particular trade felt that the cost of commercial insurance was too high relative to their particular claims experience, or that they had an insurance need which was not being met by the commercial market at that time. Contributions were made to the fund on the basis of tonnage or value and, in bad years, the members would be called upon to make additional contributions to keep the fund solvent.

Protecting and indemnity associations. Most mutual indemnity associations have now been taken over by the normal insurance market, but there is still a very healthy marine market in this area. Their survival is probably due to the fact that they are the largest and longest established and were thus not under the same financial strain as other trade mutuals. Protecting and indemnity associations, as these marine associations are called, were formed by shipowners to provide cover for certain areas of risk which were not covered in the normal marine market. These marine associations or "clubs" insure liabilities for cargo, liabilities to crew, to passengers, and to third parties. They also cover one-quarter of the shipowner's liability for damage done to another ship in collision, as the shipowner's hull policy only covers three-quarters of such liability.

Collecting friendly societies
These societies are run on a mutual basis and are formed by registration under the Friendly Societies Acts. They transact industrial life assurance and, in some cases personal accident and sickness covers (*see* Chapter Two). While some of these societies are nationally known names, the majority operate within a restricted area of their registered office. Friendly societies can issue life assurances up to £1,000 sum assured plus bonuses.

Industrial life assurance companies
Many of these companies are proprietary companies whose activities are controlled by the Industrial Assurance and Friendly Societies Acts. Premiums are collected weekly or monthly on industrial business but they usually transact ordinary branch life business (OB) also. (Premiums are collected every two months or less frequently, usually quarterly, half-yearly or yearly or if monthly by banker's order or direct debit.)

The limit of £1,000 applying to friendly societies' policies does not apply to industrial life assurance companies, who can issue policies for larger amounts.

Self-insurance
As an alternative to purchasing insurance in the market, or as an adjunct

to it where the first layer or proportion of a claim is not insured in the commercial market, some public bodies and large industrial concerns set aside funds to meet insurable losses. As the risk is retained within the organisation, there is no "market" transaction of buying and selling, but such arrangements have an overall effect on the funds of the market in general and on premium levels where the organisation is carrying the first layer (excess or deductible).

The student should note the difference between "self-insurance" where a conscious decision is made to create a fund, and "non-insurance" where either no conscious decision is made at all, or where no fund is created. Self-insurance schemes, while having certain advantages, also have some serious disadvantages.

Advantages of self-insurance
The advantages of such a scheme may be summarised as follows:

(a) premiums should be lower as there are no costs of broker's commission, insurers' administration and profit margins;

(b) interest on the investment of the fund belongs to the insured: this can be used to increase the fund or to reduce future premium contributions;

(c) the insured's premium costs are not increased due to the adverse claims experience of other firms;

(d) there is a direct incentive to reduce and control the risk of loss;

(e) no disputes will arise with insurers over claims;

(f) as the decision to self-insure is likely to be limited to large organisations, they will already have qualified insurance personnel on their staff to administer the fund;

(g) The profits from the fund accrue to the insured.

Disadvantages of self-insurance
The drawbacks to self-insurance arrangements are as follows:

(a) a catastrophic loss, however remote, could occur, wiping out the fund and perhaps forcing the organisation into liquidation;

(b) while the organisation may be able to pay for any individual loss, the aggregate effect of several losses in the one year could have the same effect as one catastrophic loss, particularly in the early years after formation of the fund;

(c) capital has to be tied up in short term, easily realisable investments which may not provide as good a yield as the better spread of investments available to an insurance company;

(d) it may be necessary to increase the number of insurance staff employed at an extra cost;

(e) the technical advice of insurers on risk prevention would be lost:

the insurers' surveyors would have a wider experience over many firms and different trades, and this knowledge could be advantageous to the insured;

(*f*) the claims statistics of the organisation will be derived from too narrow a base for predictions to be made with confidence as to future claims costs;

(*g*) there may be criticism from shareholders and other departments (*i*) at the transfer of large amounts of capital to create the fund and at the cost of dividends that year and (*ii*) at the low yield on the investment of the fund compared with the yield obtainable if that amount of capital was invested in the production of the organisation;

(*h*) in times of financial pressure, there may be a temptation to borrow from the fund thus defeating the security which it has created;

(*i*) pressure may be brought to bear on the managers of the fund to pay losses which are outwith the cover (i.e. make *ex gratia* payments), with the resultant depletion of the fund for its legitimate purposes, and thus making statistical analysis more difficult;

(*j*) the basic principle of insurance, that of spreading the risk (*see* Chapter Three), is defeated;

(*k*) the contributions made to the fund do not qualify as a charge against corporation tax, whereas premium payments are allowable.

Captive insurance companies

Captive insurance is a method of transacting risk transfer which has become more common in recent years among the large national and international companies. The parent company forms a subsidiary company to underwrite certain of its insurable risks. The main incentives are to obtain the full benefit of the group's risk control techniques by paying premiums based on its own experience, avoidance of the direct insurers' overheads and obtaining a lower overall risk premium level by purchasing reinsurance at lower cost than that required by the conventional or direct insurer.

Reinsurance is discussed in full in Chapter Ten; suffice it to know at the present time that all company insurers only retain a portion of most risks and reinsure or "insure again" the portion which is above their financial ability to retain. As the direct or commercial market insurer has all the procuration and survey costs to bear, the net cost of reinsurance is substantially less than the cost of direct insurance. Hence, the captive company can have access to the lower cost reinsurance market and, through the proportion of the risk retained, still have the advantages to the group of self-insurance for that amount of risk. The premiums paid to the captive company are allowable against corporation tax, although recently in America the IRS (the US equivalent of the Inland Revenue) have disallowed such premiums where the captive transacts no business from risks created outwith the parent company.

Several captives now transact business from other sources, and many captives are operated from offshore tax havens such as Bermuda and Guernsey in order to obtain additional savings through taxation concessions in these areas.

The state
The state also acts as an insurer, as under the National Insurance Acts all employed persons must contribute to the National Insurance scheme. The provisions of the National Insurance scheme are dealt with in Chapter Eleven.

Classification of insurance companies
In this chapter so far we have classified companies according to their form of ownership, but sometimes companies can be classified in other ways.

Specialist companies are those which underwrite one type of insurance business only, e.g. life companies, engineering insurance companies.

Composite companies are those which underwrite several types of business.

Tariff companies are those which are members of an association which governs the activities of its members by laying down minimum premium levels (hence the word tariff) and the form of policy wordings. The only association remaining is the Fire Offices' Committee (FOC) which governs fire insurance and is discussed later.

Non-tariff or independent companies are those which operate in the same market as the tariff companies, but who decide on their own policy wordings and premium levels. In practice they largely follow the tariff wordings and premium levels, but allow a discount for the better risk.

LLOYD'S

Lloyd's is probably the most famous insurance market in the world, being the centre for the world's marine insurance and shipping intelligence.

Historical development
In the seventeenth century insurance of ships and cargoes was often underwritten by merchants who were willing to carry part of the risk of a voyage for part of the premium. Commerce of various types was transacted among the merchants who met each other in various coffee

houses around the City of London. Similarly, those wishing to transact insurance would meet in these coffee houses. One of them, owned by an Edward Lloyd, was situated near the River Thames and was frequented by merchants, shipowners and others having an interest in maritime ventures.

Lloyd's Coffee House was situated in Tower Street and was in existence in 1688 although the original date of opening is uncertain. Edward Lloyd encouraged the merchants or underwriters (they signed their names at the foot of the insurance contracts) because it brought extra business to his coffee house. He supplied shipping information and in 1696 began publication of a news sheet called *Lloyd's News*. This was superseded some years after his death by *Lloyd's List* which is London's oldest newspaper.

In 1769 the insurance market transferred its business centre to the New Lloyd's Coffee House in Pope's Head Alley, and in 1771 a Committee was formed to seek larger premises. The formation of the Committee took the running of Lloyd's out of the hands of the coffee house owner (then Thomas Fielding) and into the hands of the insurance fraternity. From their membership subscriptions premises were found in 1774 in the Royal Exchange.

The modern Corporation of Lloyd's was formed in 1871 by Act of Parliament and more recent statutes have kept the constitution up to date with the needs of a modern insurance market. The present premises are centred in Lime Street, London. New premises are currently under construction, adjacent to the present site.

The Lloyd's Act 1982
Following an enquiry into the constitution and self-regulation at Lloyd's, under the chairmanship of Sir Henry Fisher, the Lloyd's Act 1982 was passed.

Under the Act the overall responsibility for the control of affairs at Lloyd's is vested in the Council of Lloyd's, which is made up of some 28 members including a number who are not actively involved in the transaction of insurance.

The Committee of Lloyd's comprises the 16 *working* members of the Council, and is responsible for the day-to-day running of affairs.

Membership
There are around 23,000 underwriting members of Lloyd's. To become a member, the applicant must:

(a) be nominated by one member and supported by other members;

(b) transact business with unlimited and personal liability (note here the favoured position of the company shareholder; in addition to his funds in Lloyd's, the member has his total personal wealth at risk);

(c) satisfy the Committee as to his integrity and financial standing;

(d) furnish security as approved by the Committee, which will vary according to the volume of business transacted: this security will be held in trust by the Corporation;

(e) pay all premiums into a premium trust fund from which only claims, expenses and ascertained profits may be paid;

(f) furnish a guarantee policy each year, subscribed by members of Lloyd's;

(g) contribute a levy based on premium income to a central fund which is for the protection of policyholders should any member be unable to meet his liabilities (the defaulting member is still responsible for his liabilities to the full extent of his private fortune);

(h) submit to an annual audit as regards solvency in the terms of the Insurance Companies Act. The auditor, approved by the Committee, submits a certificate to the Department of Trade and Industry. Current legislation only confirms an audit procedure which has been in force for seventy years.

Syndicates

Because of the complexity of modern insurance transactions and the fact that there are around 23,000 members, business is transacted by syndicates consisting of anything from a few to several hundred members. These syndicates are represented in the Lloyd's underwriting room ("the Room") by an underwriting agent (underwriter) who can sign on behalf of the syndicate. Each member of a syndicate is still responsible as an individual for his share of the insurance accepted by the syndicate. There are about 417 syndicates represented in the Room, made up of approximately 154 marine, 169 non-marine, 49 aviation, and 45 motor syndicates.

The Room

The underwriting room is a large hall with a gallery, 120 feet by 340 feet (approximately 37 metres by 105 metres). Marine, motor and aviation business is transacted on the ground floor and non-marine business generally on the gallery. Underwriters and their staffs sit at "boxes", each with a number, and the Lloyd's brokers negotiate their contracts there. The Room at Lloyd's is the only place in Britain where there is a recognised insurance market in the accepted sense of the word as described in the first paragraph of this chapter.

The Lloyd's broker

The Committee of Lloyd's, in addition to approving the appointment of members, also appoints brokers to act as Lloyd's brokers. The Lloyd's broker represents the insured in the transactions with the underwriter.

They are required to satisfy the Committee as to their expertise, integrity and financial standing. After being appointed, they can display the words "and at Lloyd's" on their letter heading and nameplates.

Although only approved brokers can enter the Room and place business, the Lloyd's brokers are otherwise the same as other insurance brokers in their dealings with insurance companies (*see* "Insurance intermediaries" *below*).

Transaction of business at Lloyd's

It was mentioned previously, and shown in the diagram of the insurance market, that only Lloyd's brokers may place insurance at Lloyd's. When requested to place insurance at Lloyd's, the Lloyd's broker will prepare a "slip".

The *slip* is a sheet of paper containing details of the risk to be insured. It will show the following:

(*a*) name of insured;
(*b*) period of cover required;
(*c*) inception date of cover;
(*d*) perils or type of cover required;
(*e*) property to be insured;
(*f*) sums insured or limits of liability;
(*g*) special conditions to be incorporated;
(*h*) expected premium.

Underwriting. The broker will take the slip to an underwriter who specialises in this class of business, with a view to his accepting the lead or first proportion of the risk. Discussions on other aspects of the risk, e.g. claims experience, will take place and the underwriter may feel obliged to amend some of the terms on the slip before he can accept the rate of premium or the conditions. Once agreement on terms has been reached the underwriter will stamp and initial the slip for the proportion which he wishes his syndicate to accept. This proportion may be very low, say 5 per cent, and the broker will proceed to other underwriters until the slip is filled, that is until 100 per cent is underwritten. If the broker establishes a good "lead", other underwriters will accept the terms of the leading underwriter, otherwise the broker has to start again on the new terms. Each underwriter will record details of the risk underwritten for his own records.

Policy signing office
When the slip is complete the broker returns to his office and has the policy prepared in accordance with the slip. The policy and slip are then submitted to Lloyd's Policy Signing Office where the policy is checked with the slip and signed on behalf of all syndicates. Accounts are

prepared monthly for the syndicates and brokers from the data recorded
at the Policy Signing Office.

Claims

The Lloyd's broker also provides a service to his client in the settlement
of claims. In the case of marine claims he negotiates with the staff of a
central office called Lloyd's Underwriters' Claims Office, and for non-
marine claims he negotiates directly with the syndicates' claims officials
at the boxes in the Room.

Lloyd's intelligence and other services

It will be recalled that Edward Lloyd started to give shipping news in his
coffee house some 300 years ago. This service has been increased
manyfold, so that today Lloyd's is the leading source of shipping
information in the world. Information is received daily from all over the
world by the Intelligence Department, who distribute the information
through the various publications and organisations listed below.

Lloyd's List is a daily newspaper dealing with matters of general
interest to shipowners and others with maritime interests. It also reports
marine and aviation accidents, arrivals and departures of merchant
shipping throughout the world, together with details of ships due to
arrive or that are in dock at selected UK ports.

Lloyd's Shipping Index is published Monday to Friday inclusive and
lists ocean-going ships alphabetically, showing type of vessel, owner,
flag, classification society, year of build, gross and net tonnage, current
voyage and last reported position.

Lloyd's Loading List is published weekly, and its monthly
supplement *Cargo by Air* provides exporters with a valuable guide to
cargo carrying services.

Lloyd's Law Reports specialise in shipping, insurance, aviation and
commercial cases heard in the English, Scottish, Commonwealth and
United States courts.

Other publications are *Lloyd's Calendar* (a handbook on Lloyd's),
Lloyd's Survey Handbook and *Lloyd's Weekly Casualty Reports*.
Casualty reports are prepared daily for all sections of the market and
displayed on notice boards in the Room.

Lloyd's Register of Shipping, which is a detailed register of survey
details of ships, is not published by Lloyd's although members of the
Committee of Lloyd's serve on the Committee of Lloyd's Register of
Shipping.

Data processing services, in addition to processing data from the
Policy Signing Office, provide data processing facilities to other
departments and other market organisations.

Lloyd's agents are situated in the leading ports and areas of the world and are the source of much of the information published. They also conduct surveys and arrange for surveys to be carried out in connection with losses and, if appointed as claims-settling agents, they can settle claims abroad. At present there are in the region of 1,300 Lloyd's agents and sub-agents throughout the world.

STRUCTURE OF A COMPOSITE INSURANCE COMPANY

In order to appreciate how an insurance company operates, it is helpful to look at the organisation from two particular aspects: the personnel and the geographical organisation.

Personnel

There is no uniformity of practice or of titles from one company to another, so that the internal organisation of any one company may not coincide with the terms and layout of Fig. 4, although all of these functions will be carried out. The functions of the personnel shown are as follows.

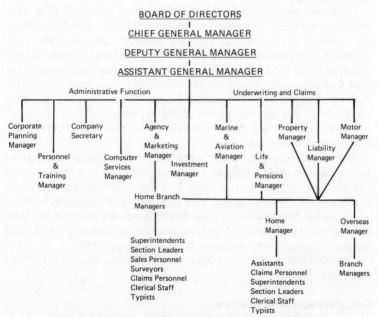

Fig. 4. *The structure of a typical insurance company (personnel).*

Board of directors. The function of the board is to formulate the overall plan of operation of the company in the best interests of the owners (the shareholders), taking into account the interests of policyholders, staff, the public and the effect of market competition. An examination of the composition of an insurance company's board will show a blend of talent—some titled persons to add prestige to the company and for the benefit of their experience in other business pursuits; prominent people from the industrial and commercial world for the benefit of their expertise; and perhaps one or two of the company's general managers for their insurance expertise.

Local boards of directors. Some companies have boards of directors attached to leading branch offices. These are non-executive directors and are appointed to promote the interests of the company locally and to give advice on local affairs to the branch manager.

General managers. The chief general manager is the chief executive of the company, and he will be assisted by a deputy and several assistants depending upon the size of the company. Each assistant will have a particular area of responsibility, and some of the administrative and underwriting managers shown on the chart may have assistant general manager status.

Corporate planning manager. The activities and costs of a large insurance company are now so vast that many of them have set up departments of specialists, e.g. organisation and methods staff, statisticians and economists, to advise on the changes in plan which will be necessary in the future. In this way it is hoped that the company can cope with change, and progress smoothly in a rapidly changing world.

Company secretary. The responsibilities of the company secretary are those of the administration of the organisation as a registered company and ensuring that the company complies with company and insurance company law.

Investment manager. In any large insurance company the reserves will amount to several millions of pounds, and this vast fund must be invested for security and income. In Chapter Three the investment portfolios of British companies were summarised. If long-term business is transacted, the company must have an actuary to meet the legal requirements and he may be the investment manager or the life manager, perhaps with assistant general manager status.

The functions of the other personnel shown on the chart is fairly clear from their titles.

Geographical organisation

The geographical organisation of a typical company is shown in Fig. 5.

Executive head office. This is usually situated in London although there are head offices in Norwich, Liverpool, Kendal, Perth, Glasgow and Edinburgh. Some companies maintain complete head offices in

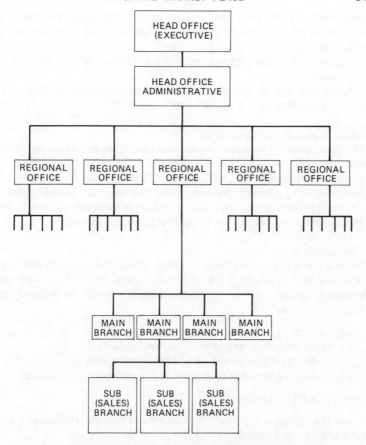

Fig. 5. *The structure of a typical insurance company (geographical).*

London, but because of the high cost of office space and salaries in London and difficulties in communication, many companies have moved the general administrative and underwriting work to a second head office in the provinces.

Administrative head office. The main burden of management and underwriting is carried out here, usually in the provinces where costs are lower. The computer centre is likely to be outside London for better telecommunications.

Regional offices. Some companies operate on a partially decentralised system (*see below*) where certain zonal or regional offices have underwriting authority for branches within their region.

Main branches. These branches are responsible for initial

underwriting within their area and that of their sub-branches. They are also responsible for claims handling (unless taken over by a regional office) and mainly for sales promotion.

Sub-branches. The prime purpose of a sub-branch is sales promotion in its area.

Not all companies operate with regional offices and this is discussed under "Decentralisation of authority" below.

Decentralisation of authority

The operational organisation of an insurance company can range from complete centralisation of all decision-making at head office to complete decentralisation with branches having wide ranging powers within broad guidelines. Between these two extremes is the regional system, whereby certain main centres are given substantial authority on underwriting and claims for the branches within the region.

Centralisation

When a company is centralised all underwriting claims, policy drafting, renewals and accounts work is handled from head office with the branches acting merely as sales outlets. Some advantages of centralisation are:

(*a*) uniformity of policy, practice and routine;
(*b*) most economic use of mechanised methods;
(*c*) fewer experts required with a resultant saving in salaries;
(*d*) branches relieved of routine work can concentrate on selling.

Some disadvantages are:

(*a*) the system is often run from an area of high salary, building and rating costs, e.g. London;
(*b*) poor service can result from the adminstration being remote from the customer;
(*c*) excessive power lies in a few hands—dictatorial attitudes can develop in underwriting to the detriment of the company;
(*d*) lack of promotion prospects for most of the staff.

Decentralisation

Under this system each main branch is responsible for its own underwriting, policy drafting and claims.

Some advantages of decentralisation are:

(*a*) local officials will best understand local conditions;
(*b*) good local service is possible;
(*c*) branch staff become more knowledgeable by having to make decisions;

(*d*) democracy is brought to the underwriting policy of the company;

(*e*) better staff morale is created by providing more chances of promotion to the higher grades of post required at the branches.

Some disadvantages are:

(*a*) many experts will be required with a higher salary bill as a result;

(*b*) branches are bogged down with routine work, instead of concentrating on selling which is their main function;

(*c*) effort is wasted in trying to make each branch expert in everything;

(*d*) divergence of practice is likely to develop between branches and this can be embarrassing if it becomes known to the public. It can also lead to misleading statistics for the company nationally.

Few companies are either completely centralised or completely decentralised and in the 1960s there was a general shift to a half-way house by way of a regional system.

Regional system
Under this system the country was divided into, say, ten regions and the principal branch became the regional office. It took over the underwriting, policydrafting and claims work from head office or the branches depending upon the system in force before. In this way an attempt was made to remove most of the disadvantages of both systems, while retaining many of the advantages of both systems.

In the latter part of the 1970s the tendency appeared to be to remove some of the authority from main branches to regional offices and from regional offices to head office. While this may appear to be a backward step it must be seen in the light of technological change and on the one hand the greater capabilities of the computer as a labour-saving device, and on the other the need to increase sales volume in order to achieve the best use of those facilities where costs cannot be reduced. The present scene appears to indicate the closure of some sub-offices; withdrawal of routine work from some main branches to make them sales offices only; and removal of routine work on underwriting, endorsements and claims to the central computer, often by means of teleprinters and visual display units (VDUs) at regional offices.

Mechanisation
Insurers have always been keen to save costs and increase efficiency by the use of the latest business techniques. Three types of modern technology are currently being used by many companies and their use will expand in the next few years.

The computer. An increasing number of branches and regional offices will be equipped with teleprinter keyboards and VDUs linked to the company's computers. They are being used extensively at present for updating accounting records and renewal records on the computer files. Some companies are preparing policies on the computer by means of codes typed on the teleprinter, and the computer translates these codes into the relevant clauses and conditions and the policy is typed via a coupled printing machine. Greater use of this facility will be made in the future.

Automatic typewriters. In cases where standard letters or documents have to be issued it is possible to programme an automatic typewriter (word-processor) by magnetic card or tape. The machine stops at predetermined places for particular information to be typed in for the individual document. Each completed document or letter appears to have been individually typed.

Modern developments. Much publicity has been given to the micro-chip which enables intricate computers (word-processors) to be made in small bulk. One of the developments in this field is a machine which can translate the spoken word into electrical impulses (voice-reading machines); these in turn instruct a printer to type the words almost simultaneously. Offices which have introduced the system have been able to reduce the size of their typing pool by up to 50 per cent. Portable machines will soon be available; one suggested use is that insurance sales inspectors will be able to issue typed quotations and even simple policies to clients at the interview.

INSURANCE INTERMEDIARIES

Members of the public can arrange insurance cover direct with an insurer, except where the cover is to be placed with Lloyd's when, as has been seen, the services of a Lloyd's broker must be utilised. However, the vast majority of the premium income of insurers comes to them indirectly through the use of intermediaries of one sort or another.

The role of the intermediary or agent

The prime duty of an agent is to bring his principal into a contractual relationship with another, and to stand in place of his principal in the performance of any functions covered or implied by the terms of the agreement. In insurance cases, the agent's function is usually to negotiate cover and terms, and in doing so he takes the place of the principal. However, the principal will be bound by actions of the agent, the legal doctrine being *qui facit per alium facit per se* (he who does something through another does it himself).

One of the best known legal cases on this point is *Newsholme Brothers v. Road Transport & General Insurance Company* (1929), where an agent filled in wrong information on a proposal form even although the principal had given him the correct information. The principal signed the form without noticing the error and when a claim was made later, the insurers were able to repudiate liability on the grounds of misrepresentation. A full discussion on the doctrine of disclosure is included in Chapter Eight.

The agent must exercise due care in carrying out his duties and it is reasonable to expect a higher standard of care to be shown by, for example, the insurance broker, than by the part-time agent (*see* "Agents" *below*). If he does not do so and his principal suffers a loss through the agent's negligence, the principal can sue him for damages. All agents owe a duty of care to their principals, but the expert agent owes a much higher duty of care.

Creation of the agency. For the purposes of this text we need only concern ourselves with three methods of creating an agency:

(*a*) orally, where the parties agree by word of mouth that A shall act for B;

(*b*) in writing, but otherwise as in (*a*) above: many insurance brokers obtain a written "mandate" from a client who wishes the broker to act for him;

(*c*) by implication, i.e. where from the conduct of the parties it may be implied that the agent/principal relationship applies.

In method (*c*), the classic insurance case is *Murfitt* v. *Royal Insurance Company* (1922) where the agent was implied to have authority to issue cover, because previous *ultra vires* actions of this kind had been ratified by the company concerned.

Whose agent? The law of agency can become rather complicated in insurance transactions. Insurers issue letters of appointment to part-time and full-time (broker) agents. The purpose of these agencies is to have the agent procure business for the company, collect premiums and handle renewals and policies. These same agents, however, are generally deemed to be agents of the proposers in the negotiations prior to the contract and in giving advice to the proposers. In the event of dispute the courts will look at the particular action the agent was performing and decide whether the agent was acting for the insured or the insurer at the time.

Rights of the agent. Agents are entitled to remuneration from their principal for their work. The historical practice within the insurance industry is for the agent to receive a commission from the *insurers* based on the premium for the contract; the general law of agency does not allow him to receive a secret profit from a third party.

The commission system can be inequitable as the agent will receive a low remuneration on good business because of the low premium and a high commission on poor business because of the high premium. In each case the premium and commission may not be proportional to the amount of work done on the case by the agent.

There is a school of thought which advocates remuneration by fee payable by the proposer and based on the amount of work done. However, it is difficult to change a system which has been in operation for hundreds of years, and it is highly unlikely that the commission system of payment will be abandoned in the foreseeable future.

Categories of insurance intermediary
As previously mentioned, all intermediaries are agents in law, but, in insurance usage, they are classified as brokers and agents.

Brokers
There are two categories of brokers:

(a) Lloyd's brokers: they are the only persons permitted to place business at Lloyd's (see above). They also place business in the company market.
(b) Other brokers (just termed "brokers").

Both categories are full-time professionals who must be registered (see below). They normally act as agents for the insured (Lloyd's brokers always so), and are remunerated by a higher rate of commission than agents. By calling themselves "brokers" they are holding themselves out to be experts in the field of insurance and have a higher duty of care to their principals than agents. They will generally have authority to issue cover for certain classes of insurance and in some cases may issue simple policies, e.g. travel and perhaps household.

The insured can obtain independent advice on a wide range of insurance matters from a broker without direct cost to himself. For example the broker will advise on insurance needs, the best type of cover and its restrictions, the best market, claims procedure, and the obligations placed on the insured by policy conditions, and he will up-date the information as time goes by to take account of market changes. From the insurers' point of view, negotiations with brokers are easier and speedier as only the intricate points or special requirements require detailed discussion, thus saving time and money on routine matters.

Agents
Although all brokers are legally agents, the word "agent" in insurance usage is restricted to the part-time agent. This type of individual or firm has some other occupation as the full-time source of income, but in the course of such business clients may require insurance cover. Examples of this type of agent are solicitors, accountants, estate agents, building

societies and garage proprietors. Almost anyone can become an agent for a company if that company feels that they are in a position to influence business being placed with the company.

A sub-category of the part-time agent is that of the "own case" agency. In this case, the only business which the agent has with the company is his own insurances, but for the purposes of procuring that business the insurer has given him an agency so that he obtains the commission by way of a premium rebate.

Unfortunately, the word "agent" is used in another connection, and that is the "industrial assurance agent". This individual is not an intermediary, but an employee of the industrial life office, and a more fitting title would be "collector/salesman". He is employed to collect the weekly industrial life premiums and sell business and is paid by a basic salary plus overriding commission.

Cash and credit terms

The majority of brokers and part-time agents are given appointments by companies on credit terms. This means cover, policies and renewal documents will be issued to them before they have paid the company, and an account listing all debit and credit balances will be issued monthly or sometimes quarterly. Some brokers and agents, very few in relation to the total number, have their accounts limited to a cash basis (cash-agents and cash-brokers), where they must pay the premium before cover is issued. Such an arrangement is more expensive to operate and the commission payable is usually lower. The reasons for such an arrangement are usually that the agent is in a very small way of business or that he has proved to be unsatisfactory in running the agency or brokerage on a credit basis.

Insurance Brokers (Registration) Act 1977

Until recently anyone could describe themselves as an insurance broker whether they had any insurance knowledge or not, and it was difficult for the public to distinguish the genuine professional expert from the "fly-by-night". At least 9,000 firms called themselves brokers (compared with many tens of thousands of part-time agents) and there were four organisations of brokers which sought to maintain varying standards of conduct for their members. These organisations were Lloyd's Insurance Brokers' Association (LIBA), the Corporation of Insurance Brokers (CIB), the Association of Insurance Brokers (AIB) and the Federation of Insurance Brokers (FIB).

It was felt desirable within the insurance broking industry that there should be one body to represent the profession and to supervise the standing and operations of those permitted to call themselves insurance brokers. In January 1976, therefore, the four associations established the British Insurance Brokers' Council which prepared proposals with the approval of the Secretary of State for Trade for the registration and regulation of insurance brokers. The proposals of the Brokers' Council became the basis of a Private Member's Bill which became the Insurance Brokers (Registration) Act on 29th July 1977.

Having achieved its purpose, the British Insurance Brokers' Council was disbanded in 1977 along with the four independent associations and the *British Insurance Brokers' Association* (BIBA) was formed.

Insurance Brokers Registration Council

Under the 1977 Act the Insurance Brokers Registration Council (IBRC) was established to govern the registration and regulation of insurance brokers. The IBRC is a legally created separate independent body from the BIBA, which is a voluntary trade association.

The Council comprises seventeen members, twelve of whom are nominated by registered brokers, with the remaining five being government nominees. The Council has drawn up a code of conduct, and committees have been established to investigate complaints and consider matters of a disciplinary nature.

Since 1st December 1981 it has been illegal for anyone to describe himself as an insurance broker if he is not registered under the Act. This, however, does not prevent anyone calling himself an insurance adviser or consultant, nor the part-time agents from continuing as before.

Registration of individuals
For an individual to be registered he must:

(*a*) hold an approved qualification (at present the only qualifications recognised for the purposes of registration are the Associateship or Fellowship of the Chartered Insurance Institute, but the Council has power to accept others); *or*

(*b*) have carried on business as, or have been employed by, an insurance broker or full-time agent for at least two companies, or been employed by an insurance company for at least five years; *or*

(*c*) hold a recognised qualification (*see above*) *and* have carried on business, or been employed as in (*b*) above, for at least three years; *and, in addition*

(*d*) satisfy the Council that he has had suitable work experience.

Sole traders, partnerships and limited companies must comply with further conditions regarding solvency, accounting practices and professional indemnity insurance cover. In the case of limited companies, at least half the directors must be registered insurance brokers and the Code of Conduct requires that all work shall be under the day-to-day supervision of registered persons.

INSURANCE ORGANISATIONS

It will be apparent from a study of this chapter that there are many different interests among insurers and their intermediaries, and a study of Chapter Two will have shown that these insurers have many and varied interests over many types of insurance. It is only natural that over the years several central associations have become established to represent common interests among insurers. A summary of the activities of the more important of their associations follows, but it should be noted that this is not an exhaustive list.

The British Insurance Association (BIA)

The BIA represents over 325 insurance companies transacting some 95 per cent of the worldwide business of the British insurance company market. The BIA sets out to represent the interests of its members by:

(a) acting as a single authoritative voice for members and as a channel of communications between them and the government, financial organisations, and the bodies which seek to consult the insurance market;

(b) conducting a public relations programme designed to improve public appreciation and understanding of insurance;

(c) studying a wide range of technical subjects on behalf of members;

(d) operating a system whereby complaints against member companies can be investigated at senior level within the company concerned.

Examples of its work in these areas either recently or currently as ongoing programmes are:

(a) submissions to the Pearson Committee (i.e. the Royal Commission on Civil Liability and Compensation for Personal Injury);

(b) submissions, jointly with life associations (*see later*), to the Commission to Review the Functioning of Financial Institutions under the chairmanship of Sir Harold Wilson;

(c) consultation with the Inland Revenue on various aspects of taxation;

(d) discussions with accounting bodies on accounting standards;

(e) representing the interest of members at the drafting stage of Law Reform Reports and statutes such as the Policyholders Protection Act 1975, the Insurance Companies Acts 1974 and 1982 and the Insurance Brokers (Registration) Act 1977;

(f) research into vehicle repair methods and costs at the Motor Insurance Repair Research Centre at Thatcham and at motor engineers units for vehicle repair at various places throughout England; and the gathering of risk statistics in the areas of motor insurance, employers' liability insurance and household risks;

(g) public relations through press advertising, schools literature, films, radio and TV interviews and press conferences mostly through the work of the BIA's regional committees and officers;

(h) consultations and conferences with the Health and Safety Executive on industrial safety;

(i) consultation with various interested parties within the EEC on the drafting of EEC Directives relating to insurance.

Marine insurance organisations

Several organisations have been formed to represent the interests of underwriters in the various marine markets. These organisations work closely with each other while representing the particular interest of their members.

Lloyd's Underwriters' Association. As the name indicates this association is concerned with technical and other matters affecting Lloyd's marine market.

The Institute of London Underwriters. This is a forum for the company marine insurance underwriters. The Institute operates a policy signing office similar to that in operation at Lloyd's. In order to simplify the placing of business among various companies and in claims settlements, it is desirable that all policies covering one type of risk have similar clauses and wordings. The standard clauses used by its members, known as the "institute clauses", are now used by the British market as a whole.

Liverpool Underwriters' Association. This Association represents the interests of marine insurers, brokers and loss adjusters operating in the Liverpool marine insurance market. It provides a shipping intelligence service and produces statistics on maritime losses.

Organisations associated with fire and fire insurance

These organisations are all concerned with protection against fire damage, or with the transaction of fire insurance, although there is some interdependency.

Fire Offices' Committee (FOC). This is an association of many of the leading company fire insurers in Great Britain. It forms the "tariff" group of companies whose aim is to pool statistical information and so obtain as sound a statistical footing as possible on which to base rating requirements for the future. It also publishes for its members a very detailed scale of minimum (but not maximum) rates for many types of trade, thus establishing a sound economical base to the fire insurance market. As in marine insurance, it is desirable to have standard policy wordings in the fire market where so many risks are shared (*see* Chapter Seven), and the FOC prepare such wordings for their members.

There is close liaison between the FOC and the "non-tariff" or "independent" offices and Lloyd's. It is sometimes argued that a monopoly has been created in the UK fire market, as the independents and Lloyd's often use the tariff-rating structure with a small discount. In spite of a recommendation several years ago by the Monopolies Commission that the rating part of the FOC should be disbanded, it is still functioning.

The reason that this has been allowed to continue is probably due to the fact that the tariff-rating structure ensures a solid financial base to the market, while the existence of the independents (a number of them are among the largest ten companies) and Lloyd's ensure that the tariff companies must not charge more than a fair and economic premium or they will be undercut.

The FOC also draft rules and recommendations for the construction of buildings, fire doors, fire protection systems, and the operation of various processes, e.g. paint spraying, storage of oils, to ensure a minimum standard of fire protection.

Lloyd's Underwriters' Fire and Non-Marine Association. This association deals with matters affecting the fire and non-marine market at Lloyd's. Its activities are not nearly so extensive as those of the FOC.

Fire Protection Association. An association run jointly by the FOC and industry and specialising in research, education and advice on fire protection matters for industry, commerce and the public. It publishes journals giving (*a*) reports on important and unusual fires for the layman, and (*b*) reports and research reports for the scientist, engineer and expert.

Fire Insurers' Research and Testing Organisation. This association runs a testing establishment to determine the reaction of material, building materials and fire extinguishment techniques under simulated fire conditions. The organisation works closely with the government Building Research Establishment with whom they previously formed the one organisation, the Joint Fire Research Organisation.

Central Fire Liaison Panels. These panels were formed by the BIA, the Confederation of British Industry (CBI) and the local fire brigades to provide on the spot advice to local industry on their fire protection problems and to provide education material locally. The Fire Protection Association has now taken over the role of the BIA in relation to the panels.

Life assurance organisations
These organisations represent the interests of their respective members

in dealings with the public and government bodies, e.g. Inland Revenue. They publish educational material for the public, and prepare codes of practice for their members. The titles of the organisations indicate their areas of activity:

(a) *Life Offices' Association;*
(b) *Associated Scottish Life Offices;*
(c) *Industrial Life Offices' Association.*

Accident, aviation, engineering and motor insurance organisations

Accident Offices' Association. A former tariff organisation whose rating and policy wording functions were terminated in 1968. It now performs the other functions of the FOC but in relation to non-fire property risks and liability risks.

Aviation Insurance Offices' Association. Represents the company aviation market including the drafting of standard policy wordings.

Lloyd's Aviation Underwriters Association. Similar to the company association but representing the syndicates in the aviation market at Lloyd's.

Engineering Offices' Association. It provides similar services to the AOA but for engineering insurers.

Lloyd's Motor Underwriters' Association. The title is self-explanatory.

The Motor Insurers' Bureau (MIB). As was seen earlier in Chapter Two, the Road Traffic Acts require vehicle users to be insured for liability for personal injuries to other road users. The intention is to ensure that all injury victims will get compensation for their injuries caused by negligent drivers. However, the injured party would have no recovery or little likelihood of one in the following circumstances:

(a) where the driver has no insurance policy;
(b) where the driver and therefore his insurer is untraced, i.e. the "hit and run" case;
(c) where the insurer goes into liquidation (in this case only a very small part of the claim is likely to be met and that may take many years to complete).

The MIB was established in 1946 by arrangement between motor insurers and the government to create a central fund maintained by the insurers, whereby victims would get compensation in the instances cited provided they could establish their claims to the satisfaction of the normal rules of civil law. It is then left to the MIB to try to recover from the driver, but this is seldom possible.

International Insurance Certificate ("green card"). Another function of the MIB is to guarantee to foreign governments the performance by British motor insurers under the terms of the insurance certificates issued by them for foreign travel.

Organisations of Intermediaries

Up to 1977 there were four organisations representing insurance brokers, the Corporation, the Association, the Federation and the Lloyd's Insurance Brokers' Association. As mentioned earlier these interests are now represented and governed by one body.

British Insurance Brokers' Association (BIBA). Over 3,800 insurance broking businesses have already become members of BIBA and many more may be expected to join, provided they meet the requirements of the Registration Council (*see above*). The activities of BIBA include the promotion of its views on proposed legislation and on harmonisation of insurance practice within the EEC, providing research services, nominating members to sit on joint committees, and encouraging the training of new entrants to the broking profession. It also provides a forum for discussion on various classes of insurance, on taxation and accountancy problems, public relations and consumer credit.

Institute of Insurance Consultants. The Insurance Brokers (Registration) Act 1977 applies only to those intermediaries calling themselves "brokers" and there are many who call themselves "consultants". They have formed the above mentioned institute to represent their interests in fighting against any more moves there might be in the future to prohibit those not registered under the Act from acting as intermediaries.

The Chartered Insurance Institute (CII)

The main purpose of the Institute is to ensure an adequate education for its members enabling them to sit the Institute's examinations. After passing these examinations and completing a satisfactory period of practical experience, members can apply to be elected Associates (ACII) and later, after further examinations and experience, Fellows (FCII) of the Chartered Insurance Institute. Education for these examinations is provided by correspondence courses run by the Institute's own Tuition Service or by commercial organisations, and by the various colleges run by local authorities on either a part-time or full-time basis. The Institute runs a College of Insurance for short full-time courses on a wide range of topics. Membership is open to all persons engaged in or employed in insurance and so is open to company personnel, brokers, and Lloyd's personnel. There are numerous local institutes throughout the country and meetings are held frequently, either on administrative matters or in the form of talks on subjects of interest, usually with invited speakers.

SELF-ASSESSMENT QUESTIONS

Select the correct option or options in each case where appropriate.

1. (a) A proprietary company is owned by (i) the directors; (ii) the shareholders; (iii) the policyholders.
   (b) A mutual company is owned by (i) the shareholders; (ii) the syndicates; (iii) the policyholders; (iv) the directors.
2. (a) All intermediaries can place business with all insurers.
   (b) Only brokers can place business at Lloyd's.
   (c) Lloyd's brokers can place business at Lloyd's.
   (d) Lloyd's brokers can place business at Lloyd's but not with companies.
3. (a) A completely decentralised structure within an insurance company is the normal form of organisation.
   (b) A completely centralised structure within an insurance company is the normal form of organisation.
   (c) In a regional or zonal structure some of the head office authority is delegated.
4. (a) Own-case agents and industrial life agents are not "intermediaries" in the proper meaning of the word.
   (b) All "brokers" must be registered.
   (c) The Insurance Brokers (Registration) Act 1977 was brought into force to protect insurance brokers from members of the public.
   (d) "Cash-agent" is a term which can only be applied to part-time agents.
5. List three insurance organisations whose purpose is to represent interests other than those of insurers.

EXAMINATION QUESTIONS

Now that you are about halfway through the book, attempt the following questions, allowing yourself no more than 30 minutes per question.

1. Differentiate between (a) pure and speculative risks, and (b) fundamental and particular risks, giving appropriate examples of each.
2. "Insurers provide a wider function than that of paying claims." Discuss this statement.

3. Outline the origin and development of one of the main forms of insurance.
4. Your local television station asks you to prepare notes for a programme on insurance in Britain. Prepare an essay explainting the composition of the insurance market.
5. Discuss reasons why successive governments have shown an interest in insurance company operations and explain the scope of the present legislation.

CHAPTER SIX

Nature and Structure of Insurance Documents

CHAPTER OBJECTIVES

After studying this chapter you should be able to:
* describe the function of a proposal form and recognise its structure;
* identify and interpret the component parts of a policy form;
* apply the principal rules of construction to insurance policies;
* explain the structure and use of cover notes and certificates of insurance, and complete them appropriately;
* explain the function, structure and legal status of renewal documents.

PROPOSAL FORMS

When any contract is being created, there must be an offer made by one party to enter into a legally binding contract, and an acceptance by another party or parties of that offer.

The proposal form is a document drafted by the insurance company to assist the proposer in making his request or offer to be insured. Such a form is not necessary in law as offer and acceptance in most contracts can be oral or in writing.

Function of proposal forms

For the sake of speed, convenience and accuracy in handling offers to be insured, it is desirable that all requests are presented in a uniform manner. For this reason insurance companies have drafted documents in the form of questionnaires for each class of insurance business. The main function of the proposal form is to record the information which is necessary to the underwriter for him to assess the nature of the risk being proposed. It was mentioned in the introductory paragraph that offer and acceptance can take place orally, e.g. over the telephone, but even if a contract has been made in this manner, it is normal for a proposal form to be completed before the policy is drafted and issued.

Sometimes a proposal is completed for quotation purposes only, and in these circumstances the legal offer will come from the insurer, leaving the insured to complete the contract by acceptance, or to reject the offer as he wishes.

Basis of the contract. Many proposal forms formerly contained a declaration that the proposal was the basis of the contract and that the insured warranted the truth of the answers contained therein, so that any misrepresentation was in breach of contract and rendered it voidable. The effect and wording of these declarations is changing and will be discussed more fully under "Utmost good faith" in Chapter Eight.

Advertising. Many proposal forms also contain details of the cover available under the company's standard policy for that class of insurance. Sometimes other types of policy available from the company are also listed. Where the form also summarises the cover it is called a "prospectus" or more correctly a "proposal and prospectus".

The use of proposal forms
In the majority of cases, insurers prefer to receive forms for the reasons already mentioned, but there are circumstances where practice or convenience demands that they are dispensed with.

Marine insurance. Proposal forms are not used in marine insurance as the use of a broker's "slip" has been in the practice in both Lloyd's and the company market for many years. An exception to this is the insurance of small pleasure craft and other minor risks.

Lloyd's. Most insurances at Lloyd's are proposed by completion of a broker's "slip". In addition to the small craft exception already mentioned it is left to the syndicate to obtain proposal forms if necessary, for example in the case of motor insurance and life assurance.

Fire insurance. Proposal forms are usually dispensed with for large risks. There are a number of reasons for this: there may well not be sufficient space on the form to describe all the property to be insured; the company will be carrying out a survey; and the broker will have summarised the relevant information in offering the risk.

Other classes of insurance. Proposal forms are usually required even for large risks, the only exceptions being some engineering and aviation risks where surveys will be carried out, and in some unusual or contingency risks when the preparation of a form might be difficult due to the varying information required from one type of risk to another.

Format
Each company has its own form for each class of business and the reader is strongly advised to obtain a selection of proposal forms for

each class of business and to compare their structure and questions. In recent years there has been a tendency for companies to shorten their forms and to draft questions in a form which requires a "yes" or "no" answer. Proposals forms contain general and particular questions.

General questions

Proposer's name. This is important for several reasons. Apart from identifying one of the parties to the proposed contract, the name can indicate the nature of the physical or moral hazard (*see* Chapter Seven). The name of a company proposing insurance may indicate the nature of their trade, or a particular name may be that of someone with whom the company does not wish to do business because of doubtful integrity. A foreign-sounding name puts the insurer on enquiry as to the insured's experience in this country. It has been found that nationals from hot climates may not be aware of the hazards of the artificial heating necessary during business hours in the UK; in motor insurance they may not be experienced in driving on the left-hand side of the road.

Proposer's address. This is an important factor in underwriting motor insurance and all risks insurance where different geographical areas present different risks of loss. It is also of course required for correspondence purposes.

Proposer's occupation. Certain occupations present abnormal hazards, e.g. miners, airline crew and jockeys in the case of life and personal accident covers; commercial travellers or representatives in the case of car insurance; and plastics manufacturers and woodworkers in the case of fire insurance.

Previous and present insurance history. If other insurers have imposed special terms or premiums, or declined the proposer or the risk in the past, it is essential for a new insurer to investigate the circumstances thoroughly before coming to a decision regarding acceptance and terms.

Claims or loss history. The underwriter will wish to know of previous losses, whether insured or not, which would be covered by the form of insurance being proposed. Many forms restrict such information to that occurring in the last three to five years.

Particular questions

In addition to the general questions discussed above, the underwriter will be concerned with certain information which is specific to the type of insurance being proposed, and each proposal form will have particular or specific questions relating to the hazards being proposed. Examples of the type of information are given below, but again the student is recommended to study a variety of forms for himself.

Fire insurance. The fire underwriter will wish to know the construction of the building, nature of the contents, type of occupation of the building by the proposer and others, and the nature of the processes being carried on.

Motor insurance. In this case the relevant information will include the use of the vehicle, age and experience of the usual driver(s), details of convictions and accidents of driver(s), whether the vehicle is garaged at night and where it is kept.

Life and personal accident assurances. The age, occupation and medical history of the life assured, his height and weight, are all relevant to the underwriting of these risks.

Subject matter to be insured. Whatever the property, potential liability or person to be insured it must be adequately described so that it can be identified in the event of loss.

Sum insured. The amount to be covered is listed against each item of subject matter listed.

Declaration

There is usually a declaration to the effect that the proposal is the basis of the contract, and that the proposer will accept the insurer's usual form of contract. If the premium is adjustable it will provide for this, and in older forms the proposer warranted the truth of his answers. This latter wording is no longer used and such warranties are now restricted to the best knowledge and belief of the proposer.

It should be noted that all proposals do not contain a declaration. The majority of fire and consequential loss proposals do not ask for a declaration to be signed. The current code of practice issued by the BIA states that in addition to any declaration being restricted to the proposer's knowledge and belief, there should be included in the proposal form, if not already in the declaration, a warning of the consquences of non-disclosure of material facts (*see* Chapter Eight).

Signature. Below the declaration (if any) and questions there are places for the proposer's signature and the date.

POLICY FORMS

After a contract had been made between the proposer and insurer, it is recorded in a document called a "policy". The policy is not the contract, but only the evidence of it. The contract existed when one party, usually the insurer, accepted the offer of the other, usually the insured or proposer. In the event of a dispute occurring it is the policy to which the court's attention will be drawn, as it is assumed that it shows the agreement or intention of the parties, unless the insured can bring evidence to show that there is a discrepancy between the policy and the contract.

Each insurer has his own standard form of policy wording for each class of insurance, although sometimes the market has agreed to use the same wording, as in marine and fire insurances. This standard policy is printed and the insurer types in the particular details of the contract in question.

The usual form of policy used is the *scheduled* policy in which the different parts of the document are segregated from one another and the particular information relating to the contract is detailed in a schedule or list.

The discussions which follow relate to this scheduled wording.

The heading

Each policy has the full name and registered address of the insurance company at the top of the first page, and this is called the heading.

The preamble (or recital clause)

This clause is the preamble to the details of the cover, and it recites the circumstances in which the policy will operate. The clause normally covers three points:

(*a*) that the business insured is the one carried on by the insured as described in the schedule of the policy;

(*b*) that the premium has been paid or there is an agreement that it will be paid; and

(*c*) that the proposal form is the basis of the contract and is incorporated in it.

The operative clause

This clause details the type of event insured against. It may be very brief, as in a life policy which is covering death only or an all risks policy which is covering loss "from any event whatsoever, not hereinafter excluded". It can be reasonably short, as in a fire policy which is covering the cost of damage by fire, lightening or explosion (subject to qualifications or exceptions). In the case of a comprehensive motor policy it can be very lengthy in view of the various types of loss or damage, or liabilities which are insured (*see* Chapter Two).

Exceptions

It would be almost impossible to grant insurance which covered everything, so although the operative clause details the events or perils insured, there are usually some instances in which the policy will not operate. These exclusions or exceptions are sometimes included immediately after the insured peril, as in a fire policy, and sometimes there is a separate section listing them as in an all risks policy.

Some of these exceptions are peculiar to the type of policy being issued, e.g. riot in a fire policy, while others apply to almost all policies, e.g. sonic bangs or radioactive contamination from nuclear fuel.

Conditions

All policies are subject to conditions whether stated in the document or not.

Implied conditions

There are four conditions which are implied by law to apply to all insurance contracts even although they do not appear in writing:

(a) that the insured has an *insurable interest* in the subject matter insured (*see* Chapter Eight);

(b) that both parties have observed the *utmost good faith* in their negotiations leading up to the contract (*see* Chapter Eight);

(c) that the subject matter of the insurance is actually in existence;

(d) that the subject matter of insurance is able to be identified.

Express conditions

These are the conditions expressed or stated in the policy. They vary from one class of business to another and can be sub-divided into (a) *general conditions* which are printed on the policy form and apply to all policies of that type issued by the particular insurer, and (b) *particular conditions* which are specially drafted and typed on to that particular policy.

(a) *General conditions* usually deal with such matters as the reinforcement of a common law provision such as misrepresentation and fraud; alterations requiring to be notified to the insurer; restrictions in cover; claims procedures; privileges to either party, e.g. the right of the insurer to take possession of a fire-damaged building or the right of a life assured to surrender his policy; contribution (*see* Chapter Nine) with other insurers of the risk; subrogation (*see* Chapter Nine); and arbitration (*see* Chapter Seven). There may also be a cancellation clause for the benefit of the insurer, and special provision as to how the insured takes care of his plant, as in engineering and sprinkler leakage insurances.

(b) *Particular conditions* may relate to extensions of cover beyond that contained in the printed policy, or special warranties (*see* Chapter Seven) may be applied to govern the manner in which the insured operates his premises.

Classification of conditions

So far we have seen that conditions can be classified or categorised as:

(*a*) express and implied;
(*b*) general and particular.

There is a further way in which conditions can be classified:

(*a*) conditions precedent to the contract;
(*b*) conditions subsequent to the contract;
(*c*) conditions precedent to liability.

Conditions precedent to the contract are conditions which must be fulfilled before the contract is valid, e.g. the implied conditions mentioned earlier.

Conditions subsequent to the contract are expressed in the contract and can be either general or particular, for example change of situation in a fire policy.

Conditions precedent to liability are expressed in the policy and deal with, for example, the claims procedure. In life assurance the express conditions of either a general or a particular nature can be classified as:

(*a*) *restrictive,* e.g. residence, occupation or war risks;
(*b*) *privilege,* e.g. days of grace, surrender, paid-up, loans;
(*c*) *special,* e.g. payment of premiums by instalments.

Marine insurance policies do not have conditions in this form. The policy wording is standard and is adjusted when necessary by the addition of "Institute clauses".

The schedule
The schedule is the part of the policy which records the details of the particular contract. All of the clauses already discussed with the exception of "particular conditions" apply to all the company's policies of that type. A typical schedule is shown in Fig. 6.

Signature or attestation clause
The policy document is prepared by the company and is signed on behalf of the company. The printed policy form usually contains the printed signature of a senior official of the company, e.g. the chairman or general manager, and normally a senior official at the branch issuing the policy will countersign or initial the policy as evidence of the company's undertaking to honour both the printed and typewritten parts of the document.

The specification
Simple policies, where the description of the subject matter insured is relatively brief, are prepared in the manner described. In the case of large industrial risks and the like, there would not be sufficient space on

FIRE POLICY

SCHEDULE	The Schedule, Specification and Policy are to be read together as one contract. This Schedule replaces any previous Schedule.

Insurer		Policy No.	
Insured			
Address			
Business			
Period of Insurance	from	to 1600 hours on	
First Premium	£	Date of this Schedule	
Annual Premium	£		

Total Sum Insured

The Property Insured   As set forth in the Specification attached to this Policy   £

Average   If the property described in any item of the Specification shall at the time of any loss or destruction of or damage to such property by any peril hereby insured against be collectively of greater value than the sum insured set against such item then the Insured shall be considered as being his own insurer for the difference and shall bear a rateable share of the loss accordingly.

For the Insurer

Manager for the United Kingdom

Examined . . . .

FOR YOUR PROTECTION YOU ARE REMINDED THAT ANY INCREASE IN RISK IS TO BE ADVISED TO THE INSURER PROMPTLY.

Fig. 6. *A typical insurance policy schedule.*

the schedule page to record all the particulars. In these instances further typewritten pages are added to the policy and these are called "the specification". A typical specification is shown in Fig. 7. On the schedule page, under the heading of subject matter insured, the reader would be referred to the "specification attached to and forming part of this policy". The total sum insured would be shown on the schedule, but the specification would show the division of this amount over the various items insured. In large insurances of this kind, there may be many additional clauses to be added and these would appear in the specification after the schedule of amounts insured.

Collective policies

Our discussions so far have been confined to policies issued by one insurer only. Sometimes, particularly in the case of industrial fire risks, the values at risk and/or the potential hazards are too great for one company to cover by itself. In these cases the broker will approach several companies in much the same manner as the Lloyd's broker approaches the underwriters in "the Room" (*see* Chapter Five). When he has obtained agreement from the companies to cover 100 per cent of

SPECIFICATION
referred to in the Schedule to Policy No.

Column Headings	The respective Columns shall be held to apply as follows:
	Plan Ref. refers to plan(s), lodged with the Insurer, of the Premises referred to in the Column headed "Address/Description".
	Column 1: The Buildings (including landlord's fixtures and fittings therein and thereon).
	Note. Where any insurance on buildings is subject to any condition of Average such insurance does not include the part below the level of the floor of the lowest storey (whether such floor constitutes the flooring of the basement or otherwise).
	Note. Buildings insured together in one item all communicate or are adjoining or are under one roof or form one risk.
	Column 2: Machinery, plant and all other contents (excluding landlord's fixtures and fittings, stock and materials in trade, motor vehicles and property more specifically insured) the property of the Insured or held by him/them in trust for which he is/they are responsible.
	Column 3: Stock and materials in trade (excluding motor vehicles and property more specifically insured) the property of the Insured or held by him/them in trust or on commission for which he is/they are responsible.
	Column 4: Miscellaneous items as specified under the Column headed "Address/Description".
	Note. The Insurer will not be liable under any Item on Rent unless the building to which the Item relates be destroyed, or damaged by the perils hereby insured against as to be rendered unfit for occupation and then only for such a proportion of the Rent as may be equivalent to the time necessary for reinstating the damage sustained, but not exceeding the sum insured thereon.
	Note. Except where specifically insured the buildings and/or contents of
	(a) small outside buildings, annexes, gangways and conveniences
	(b) extensions communicating with any of the buildings described
	are insured under the respective column headings by the Item applying to the building to which such property is attached or belongs.

Item No.	Plan Ref	Address/Description	Col. 1 Bldgs. £	Col. 2 Mchy. £	Col. 3 Stock £	Col. 4 Misc. £	Total £

Fig. 7. *A typical insurance specification.*

the value, the *leading office* (usually the one carrying the highest percentage of cover) will carry out the survey and prepare the specification on behalf of all the insurers. Details of each company's share of the sums insured, first and renewal premiums, together with a copy of the specification are sent to them. If the following companies or *co-insurers* agree to the terms of the policy, they issue a "signing slip" to the leading office giving it authority to sign on their behalf.

The leading office will then prepare and sign a "collective policy" on behalf of all the insurers on the risk. This policy is identical to any other policy with three exceptions:

(*a*) there is no heading, i.e. the company's name and address does not appear on the front of the policy;

(*b*) wherever the word "company" would normally appear in the clauses, the word "insurers" is used;

(*c*) included in the policy is a page listing all the companies on risk with their percentages of the total amounts and their individual reference numbers. These numbers are usually the policy numbers they would have used if each had issued a policy, as a record sheet must be filed in their policy registers to complete their records.

Endorsements

From time to time it is necessary to make alterations in the wording of a policy to take note of changes in sums insured, substitution of one item by another, etc. It would be costly and time-consuming to issue a new policy each time, so a sheet of paper called an *endorsement slip* is issued noting the alterations and any additional or return premiums involved. It usually shows the "future annual premium" or new renewal premium also. In the case of collective policies one endorsement is prepared on behalf of all the insurers by the leading office.

Many companies now issue a new schedule (*see above*) showing the up-to-date position, instead of an endorsement slip, particularly for policies which have several items or sections, and for motor vehicle policies.

Trends for the future

Much criticism has been levelled at the insurance industry over the years on the grounds that policies used language which the layman could not understand, and that there were many restrictive clauses in small print. Many of the criticisms were justified and attempts are being made to redesign policies. Some companies are issuing policies in booklet form instead of on foolscap or A4 paper. Most companies are printing a heading in bold type to each section of the policy and even to each condition. The layman can then see which part of the policy deals with exclusions or claims instead of having to read right through closely typed paragraphs which were only numbered.

The criticism about the form of language used is more difficult to overcome, as most of the phrases used have been interpreted by the courts at one time or another, and any change may again need a series of court cases to settle disputes on interpretation. However, several companies have made attempts to make their policies more intelligible to the layman and no doubt this trend will continue.

RULES OF CONSTRUCTION

The drafting of an insurance policy should be carried out with care as the document is the evidence of a legally binding contract. Rules of construction relate to the manner in which a contract should be construed.

Intention of the parties
The general rule in all contracts is that the intention of the parties to the contract should prevail, and this rule is also applied to insurance contracts. There is no legal requirement that the majority of contracts, including those relating to insurance, need be in writing. In other instances, however, there may be difficulty in knowing afterwards just what the intention of the parties was at inception. Insurance contracts are normally evidenced in writing by a policy so that the intention is normally much easier to establish.

Disputes do occasionally arise, usually about the meaning of a word, e.g. value. It is assumed that the policy expresses the views of both parties and the courts will interpret the policy accordingly.

Rectification
In the event of either party (usually the insured) being of the view that a mistake has arisen in the policy drafting, they can ask for the policy to be rectified. Normally the insured requests the company to correct the error and this is done by the issue of a new policy or by endorsement.

In the event of the one party refusing to alter the policy the other can apply to the courts to have the rectification made. If it can be proved to the satisfaction of the court that the policy does not express the intention of the parties, it will order the rectification to be carried out in order that the policy may truly be evidence of the contract.

Printed, typed and hand-written words
In the event of a contradiction in terms between the standard printed policy form and the typed or hand-written parts, it will be assumed that the typed or hand-written part expresses the intention of the parties in

the particular contract, and their meaning will overrule those of the original printed words. If an endorsement contradicts other parts of the contract the meaning of the endorsement will prevail as it is the later document.

Meaning of words
Words will be construed in their everyday, popular sense unless there is evidence that some other meaning was intended. The normal rules of grammar will apply and the whole policy must be treated as a single document. This means that the intention of a word in one part of the policy will have the same intention wherever it appears, e.g. in the schedule or in the specification. To emphasise this point it is useful to include an *"identification clause"* in the schedule and specification to the effect that they are all to be read as one and a word will have the same meaning no matter where it appears.

Technical words or terms are given their strict legal interpretation unless there is evidence that a different meaning was intended. In the event of any ambiguity, the policy will be construed against the insurers since they drafted it. This is referred to as the *contra proferentem* rule.

"Ejusdem generis" rule
This doctrine states that where a group of particular things has been specified followed by more general terms, the latter must be construed as being of the same kind as the specifically mentioned ones. For example in a marine policy there are listed certain perils of a marine nature which are covered and the wording carries on ". . . and of all other perils, losses, and misfortunes. . . .". It has been held that this general statement relates to maritime perils similar to the ones already mentioned.

Express and implied terms
In the event of a contradiction between express and implied terms, the express terms will overrule the others, as it is assumed that by putting the express terms into the contract, it was the intention of the parties that they should prevail.

COVER NOTES AND CERTIFICATES OF INSURANCE
Cover notes
Policy documents take some time to prepare and some evidence that insurance cover is in force may be desirable or necessary before the policy is issued. Alternatively the insurers may be prepared to issue cover, but do not have all the information necessary to prepare the policy; perhaps a survey has to be carried out, or if new premises are

involved they may not be fully completed. In other instances the insurers may be prepared to issue only temporary cover until a survey is carried out, reserving the right to cancel the cover if the survey report proves the risk to be unsatisfactory.

In all these cases the initial cover could be confirmed by letter, but as these circumstances arise many times daily it is the practice for insurers (and their main brokers/agents in the case of motor insurance) to have books of cover notes pre-printed. Only the particulars of the individual case require to be filled in, and the note signed by an authorised official. The original is given to the insured, a copy retained on the file and usually a second copy retained in the book for audit purposes.

Cover notes have the same legal status as the policy—they are evidence that there is a contract in force. It is normal to restrict the effective period of a cover note to fifteen or thirty days as the policy will be issued in many cases within the period. On the other hand, if there are outstanding matters to be cleared up before the issue of the policy, there is a chance to remind those concerned when issuing a continuation cover note at the end of the fifteen or thirty day period. If a loss occurs during the period the cover note is in force, the insurers are liable in the terms of their standard policy unless special terms have been included in the cover given.

Cover notes are used frequently in property insurance, but are used infrequently in life assurance. Occasionally temporary life cover is issued if the premium is submitted with the proposal form and the company confirm or reject permanent cover after the proposal has been considered by the underwriters. In the vast majority of life cases, the company issues a "letter of acceptance" (which legally is the offer) if the proposal is acceptable, and the proposer completes the contract by paying the first premium. In motor insurance the cover note has a special significance as it incorporates a certificate of insurance as required by the Road Traffic Acts (*see below*). Without such a certificate the policy and cover note would have no effect for the purposes of the compulsory insurance insurance requirements of the Acts. At Lloyd's the signed slip is the confirmation of cover except in the case of motor insurance where a cover note is issued.

Certificate of insurance

In circumstances when insurance cover is compulsory by law it is usual for a certificate of insurance to be required by the statute, although public liability insurance for riding establishments is an exception.

Motor insurance

The Road Traffic Acts require that where a vehicle is on the public highway, there is in force a policy of insurance covering the user's liability for third party personal injuries caused by the vehicle or its use. Section 147(1) of the 1972 Act states that the policy "is ineffective [in the terms of the Act] unless and until there is delivered by the insurer to the person by whom the policy is effected an [insurance] certificate in the prescribed form".

The certificate must show:

(a) the registration mark of the vehicle or if in unspecified form a description of the type of vehicles insured;
(b) the name of the policyholder;
(c) the inception date of the cover;
(d) the expiry date of the cover;
(e) the persons or classes of persons entitled to drive;
(f) the limitation as to the use of the vehicle, e.g. a normal private car certificate would exclude commercial travelling.

It must also certify that the insurers are authorised motor insurers for the purpose of the Act.

When the policy is prepared it is normal practice to prepare a certificate dated from the original time at which any cover note became effective and expiring at the next renewal date. It should be noted that the certificate, or cover note incorporating one, must be delivered to the insured for it to be effective as evidence, in criminal law, of the insurance.

International motor insurance cards ("green cards")
Most countries have some form of compulsory third party motor insurance and for ease of proof of having such cover when a motorist crosses borders, insurers in each country have established bureaux on the lines of the Motor Insurers' Bureau (MIB) (*see* Chapter Five) to guarantee international certificates issued by them. These certificates must be green in colour compared with the compulsory white of the normal certificate. It must show similar information to our certificate but in addition it shows the countries to which it applies.

Under EEC Directives member countries now include the minimum third party cover required by all member states in their policies so that green cards are no longer legally required for travel within the EEC. However, the extension of cover is for compulsory third party risks only and if the insured wishes his full cover he must apply to his insurer to have the policy extended at a modest extra charge. It is the custom for insurers to issue green cards in such circumstances, as negotiations in the event of an accident abroad are easier if the insured can produce it. For travel outside the EEC countries the card is mandatory, as otherwise the motorist would require to buy insurance cover locally at each frontier.

Employers' liability insurance

The Employers' Liability (Compulsory Insurance) Act 1969 establishes the requirement for insurance cover against the employer's legal liability for accident or disease to his employees. The Act also requires that the employer must display at his premises a certificate from his insurers that he is insured against such risks. The certificate must show:

  (*a*) name of policyholder;
  (*b*) policy number;
  (*c*) date of commencement and expiry of insurance;
  (*d*) wording that the policy satisfies the terms of the Employers' Liability (Compulsory Insurance) Act 1969;
  (*e*) signature of the insurer's representative.

Oil-carrying vessels

The Merchant Shipping (Oil Pollution) Act 1971 as amended by the Merchant Shipping Act 1974 provides that without a certificate of insurance in the terms of the Acts certain vessels may not enter or leave ports and terminals.

Marine cargo

Where marine cargo risks are insured under a floating cover one block policy is issued, but no policy is issued for individual sendings. Each sending reduces the sum insured until it is exhausted. Banks and consignees may require evidence that an individual consignment is insured before discounting the bill of exchange, and in these circumstances a certificate can be issued by Lloyd's or the Institute of London Underwriters to confirm the cover. *These certificates are, of course, different in essence from the ones previously described as the earlier ones are required by law whereas the marine certificate is issued by mutual agreement.*

RENEWAL PROCEDURE

Insurance contracts, with the exception of life policies and other long-term contracts such as permanent health insurance, are usually for a period of one year only. If the parties wished to enter into another contract for the next year it would be costly to issue another policy and the practice is that the original policy makes reference, either in the preamble or in the schedule, to the fact that it can be renewed. If there is offer and acceptance the same policy document can apply to each subsequent period. The duty of disclosure (*see* Chapter Eight) arises at the time of renewal and although the original document is still used, each year legally creates a separate contract.

In the case of annual policies there is no compulsion on either party to renew the contract for a further period. In the case of long-term business, on the other hand, the contract is for a specified period of years or until the occurrence of a certain event, e.g. death, but the premium is paid in annual (or more frequent) instalments. The assurer must accept the "renewal" premium if tendered, but the assured need not renew, in which case the policy will lapse, become "paid-up", or the premiums will be paid out of the surrender value until it is exhausted.

In the case of annual contracts the terms on which the company are prepared to renew may be different from those previously applying. The increased incidence and/or cost of claims on house and motor insurance has meant that the premium will very likely be increased compared with the previous year. Sometimes it is necessary to alter the terms of cover, and in recent years there have been instances of excesses (*see* Chapter Seven) being increased and sometimes cover improved, e.g. by index-linking the sums insured to the cost-of-living index.

Renewal documents
In the case of both annual and long-term contracts it is the custom for the insurer to issue a *renewal notice* approximately two or three weeks before the expiry date of the current insurance. There is no legal requirement to issue such a reminder, but by doing so the insurer is attempting to ensure that cover does not lapse due to the insured forgetting that his policy is expiring.

The renewal notice will show the insured's name, the policy number, the type of insurance, the sum insured and the premium at which it may be renewed. The renewal date is shown, together with the address to which the remittance should be sent, e.g. the company's local branch or the credit broker or agent if one is involved. There is usually a note on the renewal notice or on the remittance slip to the effect that any changes in the risk since inception or since last renewal must be intimated to the insurers.

Legal status
As already mentioned the issue of a renewal notice is a courtesy gesture; there is no legal requirement to do so. The exact legal status of the notice once issued will depend on the wording of it. If the notice merely reminds the insured that his policy expires on a certain date, it is probably just a reminder and serves no legal purpose. The insured would then offer to renew and the company could accept or reject that offer (except for long-term business where they must accept). On the other hand if the notice invites the insured to renew, it will be construed as a legal offer, only requiring acceptance by the insured.

Whichever wording is used, the practical effect is the same, as any offer can be withdrawn before it has been accepted if further information should make the insurer wish to take this course. Special considerations arise in the case of motor insurance (*see below*).

Days of grace

Although renewal notices are sent out two or three weeks before the expiry date of the policy, it is customary to allow the insured fifteen days (or thirty days in the case of some life policies) after the renewal date in which to pay the premium. This concessionary period is known as "days of grace".

If the insured pays the premium *within* this fifteen-day period the cover continues in full and if a loss has occurred between the renewal date and the date of payment, the insured will be able to recover. Should the insured intimate by word or action, either before renewal date or within the days of grace, that he does not intend to renew, the concession is lost and the policy lapses on the renewal date.

Life policies

If the renewal premium is not paid within the days of grace, the policy does not lapse immediately. A special condition called "non-forfeiture" comes into effect and the premiums are paid out of the surrender value (if any) until it is exhausted.

Policies to which days of grace do not apply

In addition to the short period policies for which renewals are not usually issued, it is the custom to expect payment of premium on or before the renewal date in the case of marine and livestock insurances. Days of grace are not given under motor renewals where the premium must be paid on or before the expiry date to obtain full cover.

Special position of motor policies

When a premium is not paid by the expiry date and a loss occurs thereafter, but within the days of grace, the insurers are in fact back-dating cover when they accept the renewal premium within the fifteen-day period. It is an offence under the Road Traffic Acts to back-date compulsory third party insurance cover and so, as mentioned in the previous paragraph, days of grace are not given in motor renewals.

As it is an offence to have a vehicle on the road without third party injury cover, it is the practice to give the insured a further fifteen-day Road Traffic Act certificate on the reverse of the renewal notice from the expiry date of his previous insurance, provided he has not insured with another insurer in the interval. These fifteen days are not days of grace, as the cover is restricted to legal requirements and applies whether the insured renews his policy or not (provided he has not insured elsewhere). If he pays the renewal premium after the due date and within fifteen days thereof the insurers issue a full annual certificate from the previous expiry date. This procedure complies with the Road Traffic Act since they are not back-dating the RTA cover which has been in force by virtue of the certificate contained on the renewal notice. They are, of course, back-dating other cover, e.g. third party property damage, and if covered fire, theft and accidental damage to the insured vehicle, but this is perfectly legitimate if the parties to the contract agree to do so.

Long term agreements (LTAs)

In order to try to retain attractive business at renewal, and also to cut down survey and other operating expenses in the long term, it is customary for insurers to offer a discount in return for the insured undertaking to renew the policy for a certain number of years. Such agreements are common in property, liability and consequential loss insurances, but are not available in motor insurances.

The usual discount is 5 per cent of the premium for an agreement covering three years. Occasionally larger discounts are given for agreements covering a longer number of years, e.g. in engineering business where the initial survey is very expensive in time, insurers try to obtain a five-year agreement to recoup their initial expenses.

Obligations

The obligations on the parties under such agreements are:

(*a*) *on the insured:* to offer to renew at each renewal date, on the same terms as applying in the immediately preceding period of insurance, for each year of a (say) three-year period;

(*b*) *on the insurer:* if they accept the insured's offer to grant the agreed discount (say 5 per cent).

Note the following:

The insurer:

(*a*) is not required to accept the renewal offer;

(*b*) can alter the premium from that charged in the previous year;

(*c*) can alter the terms and conditions from those applying in the previous years.

The insured:

(*a*) is not required to renew if (*b*) and/or (*c*) above apply;

(*b*) is committed to the revised terms if he accepts them, and they become the agreed terms for the renewed and subsequent periods of insurance.

In the event of the insured failing to offer to renew, he is in breach of contract, and could be sued for the return of discounts already received.

SELF-ASSESSMENT QUESTIONS

1. Proposal forms are used to a very limited extent in which circumstances?
2. List the questions found in most proposal forms.
3. Give examples of four questions which you would expect to find in (*a*) a fire proposal form, and (*b*) a motor proposal form, other than those mentioned in question 2.
4. What changes have been introduced recently in the declaration which the insured signs in a proposal form?
5. Describe the structure of a scheduled policy.
6. How are the conditions in life policies classified?
7. What is a collective policy?
8. Explain the terms *contra proferentem* and *ejusdem generis*.
9. What is the significance of the cover note in motor insurance?
10. Discuss "days of grace".

CHAPTER SEVEN

Insurance Practice

CHAPTER OBJECTIVES

After studying this chapter you should be able to:
* distinguish between physical and moral hazard and explain their influence on underwriting procedures;
* explain the methods used to calculate premiums under various classes of policies;
* distinguish between sums insured and limits of liability and explain how they should be assessed;
* explain the claims procedure under various classes of policy.

UNDERWRITING

The word "underwriter" had been discussed earlier in Chapter Five when procedures at Lloyd's were explained. It will be remembered that the Lloyd's broker presented details of the case to be insured on a "slip" to the representative of the syndicate in the Room. This individual assessed the risk of loss being proposed, indicated the premium and conditions required by the syndicate, and if these were acceptable to the broker, the slip was stamped and signed at the foot to indicate the percentage of the insurance being accepted by that syndicate. Hence the term "underwriter": one who signs beneath; in this case indicating his agreement to the terms of the contract.

This process of assessing the terms and conditions to be imposed on an insurance contract is known as "underwriting" the insurance, whether it be at Lloyd's or in the company market. When discussing proposal forms in Chapter Six it was seen that the acceptance of an offer to insure could be made verbally or by letter or by the issue of a cover-note. In the company market, slips are seldom used except for certain fire insurances on a collective basis, and for marine insurance (Chapter Six: "Collective Policies"), acceptance of the insurance being indicated by one of the methods just mentioned. Although no "undersigning" may actually take place the process of assessing the risk is still the same and is still called underwriting.

The role of the underwriter
The underwriter must endeavour to arrange the terms and conditions of

the cover and its price, at levels which reflect the degree of risk which the case brings to the fund by way of potential frequency and potential severity of loss (*see* Chapter Three). These terms and costs should be equitable vis-à-vis the risks presented by other clients for the same type of insurance, they should be reasonable in order that the company will attract new business, and they should be such that a reasonable profit may be expected from the pool of all similar risks underwritten by the company.

In order to come to decisions regarding these terms and conditions, the underwriter assesses two aspects of hazard—physical and moral.

Physical hazard

Physical hazard relates to the physical or tangible aspects of the subject matter of the insurance which are likely to influence the occurrence of losses. Aspects which are likely to increase the likelihood of loss, or of its severity compared with a normal case in that class, are termed poor or unfavourable physical hazards. Similarly, aspects which are likely to reduce the incidence of loss or reduce the potential severity can be regarded as good physical features. Perhaps the easiest way in which to understand these features is to give examples from several classes of insurance.

Fire insurance

Methods of construction which are liable to add fuel to a fire rather than contain it, such as timber walls or thatched roofs, would be bad features. The storage of dangerous chemicals, oils, packaging materials, or the use of naked lights such as blow-torches or even smoking, are other examples.

Good physical features would include brick or concrete fire-stop walls and metal fire doors, automatic sprinkler and alarm systems, and the segregation of dangerous processes and goods from the less dangerous areas of a factory. However, the accidental leakage of water from a sprinkler system may do more damage to some commodities than a fire would, e.g. tightly packed paper products such as books.

Theft insurance

A building having lightweight construction walls or roofs such as timber, asbestos, or corrugated iron, or normal window catches and rim latches on doors would present several poor features offering little resistance to a potential intruder. Alternatively if the contents of a building are attractive to thieves, e.g. jewellery, wines and spirits, tobaccos, non-ferrous metals, etc., the case would be regarded as being heavy in physical hazard. Combined with poor building construction it might well be uninsurable.

Strong building construction, security locks and bolts and intruder alarm systems can greatly improve what would otherwise be a poor physical risk.

Motor insurance
The use of a vehicle in areas of high traffic density such as London, Glasgow and similar large cities increases the likelihood of an accident. The use of a vehicle for certain trades is likely to mean that it is on the road for most of the day with similar consequences; examples are vehicles used by taxi-drivers or sales representatives. Cars which are costly to repair, such as a Rolls-Royce or a Mercedes, could be regarded as presenting extra hazard. Drivers under the age of twenty-five and sports cars are often regarded as poor physical risks, but it may be more correct to regard them as high moral hazards (*see later*).

Liability insurances
The use of chemicals, oils, and the creation of dusts and vapours in industrial processes represent adverse physical hazards to employees but these can be reduced substantially by protective clothing, goggles and masks, and by the use of extraction fans and ducting. Potential liability to the public is increased where work is done in customers' premises, particularly if heat is used, e.g. cutting and welding with the use of gas burners.

Marine insurances
The use of poorly equipped or maintained vessels, stowage of cargo on deck and bad packing are examples of poor physical hazard.

Life and personal accident
A history of recurring illness and hazardous occupations such as coal-mining or deep-sea diving are examples in these fields, as is a person excessively over-weight.

Moral hazard
Moral hazard is concerned with the attitudes and conduct of people. In insurance, this will be primarily the conduct of the insured, but that of his employees and society at large have an ever-increasing influence in assessing moral hazard. Moral hazard is just as important as physical hazard, if not more so, in influencing the cost of loss.

The insured
The most serious example of bad moral hazard on the part of the insured is the person who submits false or exaggerated claims. Another example where information necessary for the proper underwriting of the

risk is withheld or misrepresented either deliberately or innocently, is discussed in Chapter Eight under "Utmost good faith".

By far the most common example of poor moral hazard is that of carelessness: the insured who fails to take reasonable care to prevent loss or damage to his property, or for the safety and well-being of his employees and others. This often arises through other pressures of business and domestic life appearing to be more important, or the insured may be totally ignorant that his or her conduct is increasing the likelihood of loss. The only really satisfactory way in which to improve moral hazard is to educate the insured in the potential dangers and how to reduce them.

It is sometimes difficult to draw a dividing line between physical and moral hazard. A sports car was quoted above as an example of a poor physical risk, but a sports car cannot by itself cause more accidents than a family saloon. It is the manner in which it is driven that constitutes the hazard; most purchasers of sports cars wish to take full advantage of their potential speed, sometimes with disastrous results. Very often the existence of a present physical hazard will be the result of a moral hazard incurred at an earlier stage. For example, the physical hazard which unsafe working conditions at a factory represent may be no more than the result of a moral hazard incurred at an earlier stage where, for example, a factory had been insufficiently well planned at the outset or improperly supervised after its completion.

A final example of poor moral hazard in the insured is the arrogant or "awkward" individual. This is often evident at the proposal stage and it is likely that he will be even harder to deal with at the time of a claim. In practice it is unlikely that the insurer or broker can improve the risk and to decline the proposer may be the best course of action for all concerned.

Employees
If management/employee relationships are poor or if it is the custom in the trade that wage levels are very low, there is likely to be little incentive on the part of the employee to be careful in his or her work. In extreme cases there may be sabotage, vandalism, or wilful fire-raising.

Society
The underwriter must always be conscious of the attitudes of society at large as these can influence the incidence of claims. In recent years there has been an increasing incidence of vandalism. In certain parts of the country fires caused deliberately have been the largest single cost of any identified source of fire damage.

Insured are also becoming more claims-conscious, and the result of these trends is, in the case of house insurance at least, that rates have been increased by up to 100 per cent in the last few years in order to keep house insurance accounts in profit.

The surveyor

The proposal form or broker's slip can only give a certain amount of information, and for all but the simplest and smallest of cases it is the practice to have a survey of the premises carried out to ascertain in full detail the nature of the property or liability risk being proposed.

The surveyor will prepare a report and frequently a plan of the premises detailing the various physical and moral features of the risk, commensurate with the type of insurance being proposed. He will make recommendations to improve the risk. Acceptance of the proposal may be conditional on the insured carrying out these improvements. The report on property risks will include an estimate of the maximum probable loss (MPL) and may make recommendations regarding reinsurance (*see* Chapter Ten). There will be detailed build-up of the premium rate which is applicable to the risk.

In the case of life assurance proposals over a certain value or where the proposer has indicated some adverse medical feature in the proposal form, it will be usual to have an examination carried out by the proposer's own medical practitioner, the company doctor, or a specialist depending on the factors of the case. Normally the expense of these examinations is borne by the company.

Rating

The rate to be charged will take into account the level of cost, which experience has shown is necessary for the normal case in this type of trade, to cover average claims costs, reserves, expenses and profit. This basic or "normal" rate will be adjusted upwards for poor physical features and to a lesser extent for general moral hazard. As indicated earlier, the insured's individual moral hazard is not readily compensated by higher rates, education being the only real answer.

On the other hand, good phyical features will warrant a reduction from the normal level of rating. Discounts are allowed off premiums for sprinklers, automatic fire alarms and fire extinguishers. In the case of intruder alarms, it is unusual to allow a specific discount, but they will influence the level of basic rating and/or the acceptability of the case.

Warranties

A warranty in an insurance contact is "an undertaking by the insured that something shall or shall not be done, or that a certain state of affairs exists or does not exist". Compliance with the warranty is, in law, fundamental to the liability of the insurer. The only time when a breach of warranty does not affect the liability of the insurer in practice is when the breach was totally immaterial to the loss which took place.

The underwriter will draft warranties into policies for two main reasons:

(a) when the insured must comply with some requirement to make the risk acceptable, e.g. removal of waste materials in fire insurance or the use of certain protective devices in theft insurance;

(b) where some adverse feature was not present at the time of survey or some advantageous feature was present and these factors have been recognised in fixing the rate—for example, in fire insurance, if no oils were stored or if fire doors were provided (these can divide a single risk into two different types of risk).

Excesses and franchises

In instances where it seems likely that several small losses could arise or where it is deemed necessary to make an insured more cautious regarding the prevention of losses, the underwriter may apply an excess or a franchise to the policy.

(a) *Excess:* the policy wording excludes the first £x of loss or of claim.

(b) *Franchise:* the policy wording excludes any payment up to £x but if the loss is more than this figure the loss is paid in full.

The former is commonly used in motor, storm, burst pipe and personal accident and illness, and the latter in marine (percentage particular average) policies issued before 1982, and sometimes in illness insurances.

SUMS INSURED AND LIMITS OF LIABILITY (OR INDEMNITY)

Sum insured

The sum insured is:

(a) the maximum liability of the insurer;

(b) the amount upon which the premium is based by the application of the rate for the risk.

It should be noted that in property insurances it is *not* the amount which the insurers promise to pay in the event of loss (as the loss may only be partial) nor, except in a few rare cases, is it an admission of the value of the property insured.

Valued policies. The exceptions just mentioned are where, because of the unique type of property involved, it might be difficult to arrive at a value after loss. In order to avoid disputes the parties agree on the value at inception, and the sum insured represents this agreed value. In the event of total loss the insurers undertake to pay that value. In the case of partial loss the claim is settled on an indemnity basis (*see* Chapter Nine) as for other property losses. Examples of policies of this type are those insuring works of art and vintage motor cars.

Life and personal accident policies. Such policies on one's own life or on the life of one's spouse are not contracts of indemnity (*see* Chapter Nine) in that the assured is assumed to have an unlimited interest in the life assured. There can therefore be no question of the assured losing less than the sum assured in the event of death, and so in the event of a claim the full sum assured is paid.

How to assess the level of the sum insured

In compiling the basic rate for a property insurance the insurer assumes that the sums insured represent the values at risk and calculates the past claims costs as a percentage of these sums or values. If the insured fixes the sum insured at less than the value at risk, then the application of the normal or basic rate will result in that insured making a lower contribution to the general fund than is commensurate with the risk being run. This may not be apparent at first, but if the reader will consider for a moment that the probability of a total loss is much less than the probability of a partial loss, then it can be seen that whereas the insurer will be fully liable for the numerous partial losses, the low sum insured only limits his liability in the event of a rare total loss. This aspect of under-insurance is dealt with later under the heading of Claims but it may be advisable to illustrate the effect on the premium of under-insurance.

Example

Value at risk: £10,000
Policy (*a*) full sum insured: £10,000
        Premium £10,000 × rate (say £0.25%) = £25.00
Policy (*b*) sum insured: £7,500
        Premium £7,500 × £0.25% = £18.75

In each case the vast majority of claims will be less than £7,500 each and the reduction of £6.25 in premium is statistically very much higher than is warranted by the likely incidence of claims over £7,500. From the insured's point of view a much more serious matter is that he is totally uninsured for the last £2,500 of value, and as will be seen later he is likely to be required to bear 25 per cent of all losses up to £7,500 due to the operation of average.

The sum insured should be fixed at a level which represents the insured's insurable interest (*see* Chapter Eight) or potential loss subject to the terms of the contract arranged, e.g. strict indemnity or reinstatement (new for old) as described in Chapter Nine.

Finally the insured must be aware that the value of property to him is continually changing, particularly in times of high inflation levels, and frequent adjustments in his sums insured will be required.

First loss insurances. Sometimes the value at risk is very high compared with any likely single loss and the insured would be reluctant to insure for full value. It is unlikely that thieves could empty a warehouse full of wines and spirits valued at £2,500,000 and the insured may only wish cover for £500,000 representing the maximum first loss which he feels he could lose. In these circumstances insurers would be prepared to issue a "first loss policy" with a sum insured of £500,000 based on a value at risk of £2,500,000, at 80 per cent or 90 per cent of the premium required for a full-value sum insured.

Limits of liability

With the exception of employers' liability insurances, which usually give unlimited liability, it is usual for liability policies to have a limit of liability for any one occurrence and either to be unlimited for any one year or to have an aggregate limit of liability any one year.

The insurers will pay up to this occurrence limit in aggregate for all claims intimated and arising out of the one event. In fixing the occurrence limit the insured must be conscious of the number of claims which could be received from various parties and the ever-increasing level of court awards for injuries received. Many policies have limits of £100,000 or £250,000 any one occurrence, but it is likely that a minimum level of £500,000 will be required in the near future, with a figure several times this level if there is the possibility of serious injury to several people from the one event.

Property policies. A few types of property insurances have limits of liability rather than sums insured. The principal ones are motor, engineering and money. In motor insurance, damage to the insured vehicle is covered by a limit of liability. In engineering policies it is common to insure the property risks and the liability risks under one limit of liability. Subject to the limit the property claims would be settled on an indemnity or new for old basis as the case may be. It should be noted that while the level of the sum insured normally has a proportional effect on the premium, different limits of liability, while having an effect on the premium, do not have a proportional effect.

Reinstatement of sum insured

Reinstatement is mentioned later (*see* Chapter Nine) as a method of providing indemnity but in relation to the sum insured it refers to cases where partial losses have been paid and the amount of the loss deducted from the sum insured. Reinstatement of the sum insured does not apply in life assurance or personal accident policies but in other cases the position is as follows:

(a) *Fire insurance.* The sum insured is reduced by the amount of any claim and must be increased, if desired, and a pro-rata premium paid. Where small losses are involved insurers often reinstate the sum insured free of charge.

(b) *Non-fire property insurance.* Again the sum insured is reduced by the amount of any loss and must be reinstated. This does not apply to glass policies where there is no sum insured, nor to money policies for the same reason.

(c) *Liability insurance.* Reinstatement of the limit of indemnity would only apply where there was an aggregate limit, i.e. "250,000 any one year of insurance". In such a case loss payment would be deducted from it and the insured may well have to consider additional cover.

(d) *Marine.* Partial loss payments are not deducted from sums insured under a marine policy and therefore several independent sums can be paid that, in aggregate, may even exceed the sum insured. Where there has been unrepaired damage and then a total loss, all within the same period of insurance, the insured will only receive the total loss payment. Where the total loss follows on from unrepaired damage but occurs in a subsequent period of insurance the insured is entitled to both the total loss and the reasonable cost that would have been incurred in dealing with the unrepaired damage.

(e) *Pecuniary insurances.* No reinstatement of sum insured is possible in the case of fidelity guarantee insurance but in consequential loss insurance the sum insured must be reinstated.

PREMIUMS

The premium, or contribution to the fund, which an insured pays will take into account:

(a) the normal rate for this type of business;

(b) the peculiarities of the risk which differ from the norm; and

(c) the maximum potential cost to the insurers of the individual case being underwritten.

Calculation of the premium

Rate per centum of sum insured. Most types of policy are costed by applying a rate per £100 to the sum insured to arrive at the premium. Examples of policies rated in this way are fire, theft, all risks, consequential loss, life and marine. The rating tables used have often been devised several years ago and may not give an adequate level of rating in the light of today's incidence of claims and the effect of inflation on them. In these circumstances, adjustments are made to reflect the experience and sometimes market competition.

It was noted above when discussing rating that the basic rate included a loading to cover expenses. The application of such a composite rate to the sum insured can mean an inequitable contribution to expenses as sums insured rise, as the costs of obtaining the business and maintaining it do not necessarily vary with the size of the sum insured. Large cases may sometimes be charged at a reduced rate as in the fire and theft markets. Alternatively, many life companies only include a measure of costs in the rate percent and add a policy charge, of say £5 irrespective of the size of the sum insured to contribute towards the said expenses.

Flat premium. In cases where there are limits of liability instead of sums insured it is often the practice to charge a level or unit premium for the risk. The most common example is motor insurance, where the basic or unit premium for a medium-sized family car in a particular town may be £250. Reductions can be obtained for claims-free driving, the most common scale being 30 per cent, 40 per cent, 50 per cent or 60 per cent for one, two, three, four, or more years without a claim. Other discounts are available for restricted driving and for bearing the first £25 or £50 of damage to the car. Certain public liability and goods-in-transit policies are also charged on a flat-rate premium basis.

Liability policies. Some public liability and all employers' liability policies are rated on a percentage basis on the annual wage expenditure for the different categories of employee. The rate charged will reflect the risk of injury or disease to the employee or public. This might vary from $2\frac{1}{2}$p per cent for clerical workers to £5 per cent or higher for hazardous occupations.

Other methods. These methods of premium calculation are by no means an exhaustive list. For example, money in transit risks are changed at a rate per mile on the annual amount of the money in transit. Indeed, any method of rating which takes account of variations in risk can be used. In commercial vehicle insurance, the type of licence, carrying capacity or seating capacity are all factors having a bearing on the premium charged.

Adjustable premiums. Frequently the exact nature of the risk to be run in the coming year can only be estimated at inception, as the volume of business or work done will vary from year to year. In these circumstances the initial or renewal premium is based on an estimate of the level of the rating factor, and the insured undertakes to give a return at the end of the year of the expenditure, value, etc. Examples of such insurances are employers' liability (wage expenditure); fire insurance on stock (stock values per month); contractors' works damage (final value of contract); money insurance (annual carryings).

Long-term agreements. Premiums will be reduced by any discount which applies to a long-term agreement (*see* Chapter Six) if one is in existence.

Cancellations of policies

Normally a contract can only be cancelled by one party in the event of a fundamental breach of the contract by the other. The breach must be in respect of a major point in the contract and not some minor point. So far as insurance contracts are concerned the breach would require to be concerned with a lack of insurable interest (*see* Chapter Eight) or a major breach of utmost good faith (*see* Chapter Eight) in which case the contract would be void *ab initio*. If this were the case the insured would be entitled to a full return of premium unless fraud or wilful deception was involved.

In other cases, once the company are on risk the premium is generally regarded as fully earned, since a total loss could have occurred, and therefore no return is legally enforceable. Insurers take a lenient view when property is sold and in several other instances. In many types of policy the insurers have inserted a *cancellation clause* giving them the right to cancel, and to return a portion of the premium to the insured.

Summary of the instances of when a return of premium is given is shown below.

Total return
A total return is given if:

(*a*) *The insurer acted "ultra vires",* i.e. if they purported to issue a class of policy for which they were not authorised in their memorandum of association;

(*b*) *there was no "consensus ad idem",* i.e. the parties were under a misapprehension or misunderstanding regarding the details of the contract;

(*c*) *the nature of the contract was illegal,* unless the insured was aware of this fact or should have been aware of it at inception;

(*d*) *there has been a breach of one of the conditions precedent to the contract* (*see* Chapter Six). If the breach was wilful or fraudulent there would be no legal entitlement to a return.

Partial return
A partial return is given if:

(*a*) *the policy contains a cancellation clause* and the insurer exercises his right to cancellation: these conditions usually allow for a "pro rata" or porportioned return to be made;

(b) *there has been double insurance:* this would apply where the insured innocently covered more than the total value of his property with two or more insurers; a return premium in respect of the excess value above the amount of insurable interest would be agreed among the insurers;

(c) *the insurer goes into liquidation,* in which case a pro rata return is given, but it is unlikely that the liquidator will have funds to pay 100 per cent in the £ of the return due;

(d) *there is mutual agreement to do so*: this could arise in the following circumstances—

  (i) if the insurer agrees to a request from the insured to cancel the insurance, or reduce the sum insured;

  (ii) where the policy is written on an adjustable premium basis (*see above*).

Short-period premiums

The comments made previously relate to annual contracts, but occasionally a policy is required for a period of less than twelve months. If the normal rating structure is used, the insurers will not receive the full loading for expenses if a pro rata premium is charged, and yet their costs will be more or less the same as for a twelve-month policy.

In some instances, e.g. fire department policies, the insurers calculate the annual premium, the pro rata premium, and 5 per cent of the difference between the two is added to the pro rata premium to arrive at the short period premium.

For example:

Annual premium	£20.00
Pro rata for three months	5.00
Difference	15.00
5% thereof	0.75

The short-period premium would therefore be £5.75.

In other cases a certain proportion of the annual premium is charged for a month or three months or whatever. For risks of six or nine months it could be that the full year's premium is charged. This is usually where there may be seasonal increases in risk, e.g. the number of motor vehicles on the road in summer months, or where experience has shown that the incidence of claims on short-period policies is proportionately higher than that on annual policies.

Minimum premiums

It is usual for a company to have a minimum premium for each class of business which reflects the cost of putting the case in the books. In recent years there has also been a trend to attempt to force more realistic sums insured to be fixed by having a fairly substantial minimum premium, e.g. several companies now have a minimum of £10.00 for house contents insurance and the same for the buildings

CLAIMS PROCEDURE

The purpose of an insurance contract is to provide an indemnity (*see* Chapter Nine) or compensation in the event of the insured event taking place, and just as the insurers have devised proposal forms and an underwriting system to ensure a convenient and competent method of initiating contracts, they have set up claims departments to negotiate and process claims in a similar manner.

Notification of claim

Almost all policies require the insurer to be notified immediately of any event which could give rise to a claim under the policy, and the insured has often to provide full particulars within a stipulated period, say seven, fifteen or thirty days. It is essential that the insurer be notified as soon as possible in order that a full investigation of the circumstances can be made. If this is not done speedily, certain evidence may not be available, or witnesses' recall of the incident may become muddled. In many cases it is in the insured's interest to have the assistance of the insurer's claims officials or independent loss adjusters to help in preventing further loss and in speeding up the start of repairs. Although the initial intimation should be in writing, this requirement is usually waived and the insurer will act on a verbal communication.

In almost every case a claim form is sent to the claimant for completion, and this will elicit information regarding the insured, the place of loss, the nature of loss, the time, a description of the property (if any) and its value at the time, and particulars of other insurances (other than life polices) covering the event for the insured's interest.

Proof of loss

The onus is on the insured to prove:

(*a*) that he suffered a loss due to an event against which he is insured;

(*b*) the value or amount of that loss. (In the case of employers' and public liability claims the insurers take over the negotiations immediately and the insured will not be concerned with the amount directly.)

If the insurers wish to rely on some exclusion in the policy, the onus is on them to prove that the exclusion applies.

Insurers are liberal in the amount of proof they require, particularly in the case of "lost" property, unless they are suspicious that fraud is involved.

Investigation of claim

If the amount being claimed is relatively minor (the amount will vary from company to company), a cheque will normally be sent on receipt of the completed claim form and satisfactory proof of value or cost of repair. In motor vehicle damage claims, the insurer's own motor engineer, or an independent one if they do not employ one of their own in that area, will inspect the damage and agree terms with the garage personnel. A similar procedure is used in engineering claims. In other property cases, it is usual to appoint a firm of loss adjusters (*see* Chapter Three) to investigate the claim and make recommendations regarding payment.

In liability claims, the insurer's own staff generally negotiate with the third party or their solicitors, unless the case is going to be fought in the courts when the insurer will appoint solicitors and, if necessary, counsel.

Average clauses

The word "average" in insurance has two meanings depending on whether one is dealing with marine insurance or other property insurances.

Marine insurance

Here the word "average" means "partial loss" and it is qualified by the word "particular" or the word "general".

(*a*) *Particular average* refers to a partial loss affecting one particular interest, e.g. the hull or a particular consignment of cargo. The policy may exclude or "be free of" particular average meaning that partial losses affecting the individual, rather than all involved in the maritime venture, are excluded. Sometimes partial losses under a certain percentage, say 3 per cent or 5 per cent of value, are excluded. New cargo wordings available since 1982 do not contain this clause.

(*b*) *General average* refers to a loss which is partial when looked at from the total values at risk in the adventure (although it could be total for one individual). If this loss was incurred voluntarily in order to save the whole venture, and this sacrifice was successful in so doing, then all parties to that venture will share the loss.

Non-marine property insurances

Here the word means to share the loss and is a device used by insurers to combat under-insurance. If there is an average clause on the policy the insured will, or may become, an insurer for the proportion under-insured, and share in contribution. The most common forms of average clause are given under the three headings which follow.

Pro rata condition of average. This is applicable almost universally to fire and theft policies.

If a sum insured is low compared with the value at risk, the insured will have contributed too little to the common pool, i.e. sum insured × rate per cent instead of value × rate per cent. In order to correct this imbalance, policies subject to the pro rata condition will only pay such proportion of the loss, as the sum insured bears to the value at risk, i.e.

$$\frac{\text{Sum insured}}{\text{Value}} \times \frac{\text{Loss}}{1}$$

Where first loss insurances are arranged (*see above*) the sum insured cannot be used as it had been agreed that it will be substantially lower than the declared value at risk. However, the latter is a factor which the underwriter takes into account in fixing his rate, and average is sometimes incorporated into these insurances on the basis of:

$$\frac{\text{Declared total value}}{\text{Actual total value}} \times \frac{\text{Loss}}{1}$$

subject to the limit of the first loss sum insured.

The special condition of average. Here a 75 per cent condition of average is applied to agricultural produce at farms. In this case the insured will share in the loss only if the sum insured is less than the stated percentage, i.e. 75 per cent of the value as insured (i.e. indemnity) at the time of the loss. If average does apply it is the pro rata condition as dealt with immediately above which applies. A similar form of the application of average applies in reinstatement insurances (*see* Chapter Nine) where the percentage is 85 per cent.

The two conditions of average. This clause is used for fire insurance on stock in certain warehouses. It would be applied to an insurance covering stock in several situations or of several types, when there was a possibility that other policies might be in force covering more limited situations or more limited types of stock. The second condition states that the wider ranged policy does not insure what is more specifically insured by the narrower ranged ones, and for the application of pro rata average as stated in condition one, the value at risk is construed accordingly. The more specific policies must deal with the loss first. The formula is:

$$\frac{\text{Sum insured}}{\substack{\text{Value at risk (less values} \\ \text{covered by more specific} \\ \text{policies)}}} \times \frac{\substack{\text{Balance of loss not paid} \\ \text{by more specific policies}}}{1}$$

Average can only be applied to insurances subject to the doctrine of indemnity (*see* Chapter Nine) and which have a sum insured.

Claims payment

Except in liability cases, when payment is made direct to the third party and solicitors, most claims are settled by payment to the insured. In rare circumstances the insurers may exercise their option to repair or replace, but this is discussed in Chapter Nine when dealing with indemnity. If payment is not made to the insured, it may be made:

(*a*) to his legal representative, e.g. in death claims, or when a person is a minor, or bankrupt or of unsound mind;

(*b*) to any person to whom the insured has assigned the proceeds of the policy, e.g. he may instruct the insurers to pay the building firm direct in the case of building repairs;

(*c*) to another party by order of the court—by a garnishee order—but this is rare.

Claims agreements

It frequently happens that an insured has a right of recovery under his policy and also from a third party by way of tort, statute, custom of trade, or contract. In these circumstances the insured will usually intimate the claim to his company and subrogate (*see* Chapter Nine) to them his rights against the third party. Alternatively he may recover from the third party and so be denied his claim against the insurer because of the doctrine of indemnity (*see* Chapter Nine). Again, he may be insured against the event by more than one company, i.e. there may be contribution among the insurers (*see* Chapter Nine).

In order to simplify the settlement of claims among insurers, various agreements have been made as to how such incidents will be apportioned or shared between them, without regard to their legal position. These agreements make for speedy settlements among companies without the need to resort to the courts for decisions and so keep down the level of premiums in the long run. The agreements are between insurers and must not prejudice the interest of their respective insured. Examples of such agreements are:

(*a*) vehicle damage repairs—the well known "knock-for-knock" agreement whereby each insurer pays his own vehicle's repair costs;

(*b*) third party sharing agreements for personal injuries in motor and employers' liability claims;

(*c*) apportionment, or non-apportionment, as the case may be, in fire losses.

"Ex gratia" payments

This is a payment out of grace or kindness, and not out of legal obligation under contract. Sometimes policyholders have no legal right to a claim payment because the event causing loss or the property damaged or lost are outwith the scope of the policy. Occasionally, however, where the decision on liability was a borderline one, there was some genuine oversight, hardship would be created, or the case involves a well-valued client or broker, a payment or part payment will be made to ensure the good name of the company.

Such payments should be made sparingly as the insurer is in a sense a trustee of the common pool to be used for paying claims covered by the policy. However, the courts have sanctioned ex gratia payments, likening them to advertising (*Taunton* v. *Royal Ins. Co.,* 1864).

Claims disputes

It is inevitable that from time to time disputes regarding claims will arise between the insured and the insurer. These disputes can involve:

(*a*) the question of whether or not the insurer is liable at all; and/or
(*b*) if so, how much that liability is.

When such disagreements arise, the claimant is usually seen by a claims official or the independent loss adjuster, and in the vast majority of cases the matter can be negotiated or explained to the reasonable satisfaction of both parties. As a last resort in cases of dispute as to liability, the insured may sue the insurer in the courts, where a decision may be made.

Arbitration

Most property policies, but not those covering life, personal accident or liabilities, contain an arbitration condition which restricts the insured's basic right to go to law on a dispute regarding amount. In such circumstances if liability has been admitted, the case must be heard by an independent arbitrator. Although the case will not be heard in court, nor by a magistrate or judge, the judgement is nevertheless legally binding on both parties, except in rare circumstances which usually involve malpractice regarding the handling of the hearing or in making the decision.

Most policies incorporating an arbitration condition state that the procedure shall be in accordance with the legislation on the point. In

England and Wales this is currently the Arbitration Act 1979 which allows for the parties to agree on a person to act as arbitrator, or if they cannot agree for the courts to appoint a suitable person. Insurers have deemed such a condition desirable on the following grounds:

(a) *Speed*: court hearings may not be possible for many months, whereas, arbitration hearings can take place within a few weeks.

(b) *Expert judgement*: where a dispute is about amount or value it is unlikely that a judge will be expert in this area, whereas the arbitrator agreed upon is likely to be an expert in the valuation of the type of property involved, and so a fairer judgement is likely.

(c) *Privacy*: the hearing will be in private rather than open court and so the insurer is less likely to receive bad publicity in the press.

(d) *Cost*: it is often argued that it will be less costly than a court hearing, but counsel will often be employed and the saving may not be great.

In spite of the aforementioned advantages the system has one major drawback, and that is that the public at large do not trust arbitration and would much prefer to have a court decision. The procedure is seldom used in practice, possibly due to the excellent work done by loss adjusters in arranging amicable settlements in difficult cases, and perhaps to a lack of knowledge on the part of the general public that they can have recourse to such a hearing.

Occasionally the insurers may waive their rights under the condition and allow the case to go to court, on the question of the legal interpretation of a certain word, e.g. value. In recent years there have been one or two cases which have gone to court on this point, and there may be more in the future, as inflation has created wide gaps between market value and reinstatement costs in building assurances. This aspect is discussed more fully under "Indemnity" in Chapter Nine.

The Insurance Ombudsman Bureau
As an alternative to the arbitration condition, several insurers have joined a scheme whereby policyholders insuring in their personal capacity may have a dispute referred to an independent Ombudsman. Before using this scheme the policyholder must have exhausted the normal channels of negotiation at branch and senior company management level. The matter must be referred within six months of the disagreement and must not be in relation to actuarial matters nor industrial life assurance. The Ombudsman's decision is binding on companies up to £100,000.

Personal Insurance Arbitration Service (PIAS)
Several companies do not agree with the Ombudsman scheme and

some of them have an agreement with the Chartered Institute of Arbitrators for them to arbitrate in personal claim disputes. In many regards the two schemes are similar, but in the PIAS the maximum liability of each individual member company varies from one class of business to another in the range £25,000 to £100,000.

SELF-ASSESSMENT QUESTIONS

Attempt the following questions and then refer to the appropriate paragraph to check your answer.

1. Distinguish between moral hazard and physical hazard.
2. Define a "warranty".
3. What is the sum insured?
4. How are premiums calculated?
5. In what circumstances is a return of premium allowed to the insured?
6. Distinguish between the following:

   (*a*) particular average;
   (*b*) general average;
   (*c*) pro rata average;
   (*d*) special condition of average;
   (*e*) two conditions of average.

7. What are the advantages of arbitration?

CHAPTER EIGHT

Basic Doctrines I

CHAPTER OBJECTIVES

After studying this chapter you should be able to:
* explain the concept of insurable interest and apply this to the main classes of insurance;
* define the basic principle of utmost good faith, describe the ways in which the principle is commonly modified, and indicate applications of the principle to the main classes of insurance;
* define proximate cause and give examples of its practical application in insurance.

INSURABLE INTEREST

We have already seen in Chapter One that insurable interest was one of the features of insurable risks. In a moral sense, if not legal, it does seem wrong for a person to be able to effect a policy of insurance on property, for example, where he does not stand to suffer in any way should the insured-against peril actually cause damage. What we will now go on to look at is the doctrine of insurable interest and try to discover the rationale behind the principle, the way in which the law has assisted its development and how it is applied to the main forms of insurance.

Rationale and definition

As we saw in Chapter Six, insurance policies are evidence of contracts that exist between the insurer and insured. The contract is one whereby the insurer agrees to indemnify the insured should a particular event occur or pay him a specified amount on the happening of some event. In return for this promise to pay the insured has agreed to pay the premium. The *subject matter of insurance* can be any form of property or an event that may result in a loss of a legal right or creation of a legal liability. In this way the subject matter of insurance under a fire policy can be buildings, stock or machinery; under a liability policy it can be a person's legal liability for injury or damage; with a life assurance policy the subject matter of insurance is the life being assured; in marine insurance it can be the ship, its cargo or the shipowner's legal liability to third parties for injury or damage.

Chapter Two outlined the scope of insurance and it may be useful to refer back to that chapter to see if the subject matter of insurance for each class of business can now be identified.

Subject matter of the contract

It is now extremely important to grasp one fundamental fact which may appear, at first, to be paradoxical. By this we mean that it is not the house, ship, machinery, potential liability or life that is insured. It is *the pecuniary interest of the insured* in that house, ship, machinery, etc. which is insured. The *subject matter of the contract* is the name given to the financial interest which a person has in the subject matter of the insurance. This concept is at the root of the doctrine of insurable interest and was expounded very clearly in the case of *Castellain* v. *Preston* (1883) in these words: "What is it that is insured in a fire policy? Not the bricks and materials used in building the house, but the *interest* of the insured in the subject matter of insurance". This is one of those quotations that is well worth committing to memory as it conveys in a few words a very complex concept.

Definition

There is no one universally accepted definition of insurable interest but what we can do is look over statutes and previous cases and try to identify what the legislature and courts have considered to be the important points. One definition is that insurable interest constitutes "the legal right to insure arising out of a financial relationship, recognised at law between the insured and the subject matter of insurance".

Essential features

By expanding upon our definition it is possible to identify the essential features of the principle, namely:

(*a*) there must be some property, rights, interest, life, limb or potential liability capable of being insured;

(*b*) such property, rights, interests, etc., must be the subject matter of insurance;

(*c*) the insured must stand in a relationship with the subject matter of insurance whereby he benefits from its safety, well-being or freedom from liability and would be prejudiced by its damage or the existence of liability;

(*d*) the relationship between the insured and the subject matter of insurance must be recognised at law.

The addition of the fourth point above is not without good cause. The case of *Macaura* v. *Northern Assurance Company* (1925) serves to emphasise the need for it. Mr Macaura effected a fire policy on an amount of cut timber on his estate. He had sold the timber to a one-man company of which he was the only shareholder. A great deal of the timber was destroyed in a fire and the insurers refused to meet the claim on the basis that Mr Macaura had no insurable interest in the assets of the company of which he was the principal shareholder. A company is a separate legal entity from its shareholders and what was being established by the case was that the relationship between the timber and Mr Macaura, whereby Mr Macaura stood to lose by its destruction, had to be one recognised or enforceable at law. In this case such a relationship did not exist as Mr Macaura's financial interest in the company as a shareholder was limited to the value of his shares, and he had no insurable interest in any of the assets of the company.

Statutory background
The fact that it seemed unjust to allow people to effect policies in respect of risks where they had no legally recognisable financial involvement had not escaped the attention of the courts. For some time prior to the Revolution in Britain of 1688 the practice had been for courts to refuse to enforce claims made under policies that appeared to conceal some gambling transaction. By the end of the seventeenth century and into the early part of the eighteenth century this general rule was relaxed and precedents were being set where the validity of "wager policies" was established. The common law was apparently failing to stop an unsatisfactory practice and legislation followed to remedy this.

Marine Insurance Act 1745
This Act forbade the issuing of policies on British ships or on "goods, merchandises or effects laden or to be laden" on them where no insurable interest existed.

Life Assurance Act 1774
The 1745 Act only related to marine insurance and it was still possible to gamble on lives and other events. The Life Assurance Act 1774, sometimes referred to as the Gambling Act, was introduced and it forbade the making of any policy "on the life or lives of any person or persons, or on any other event or events whatsoever, wherein the person or persons for whose use, benefit, or on whose account such policy or policies shall be made, shall have no interest, or by way of gaming or wagering".

The Act was not limited to life assurance as can be seen from the above quotation but "ships, goods and merchandises" were specifically excluded from its terms. One further provision of the Act was that the name of the person for whose benefit or on whose account the policy was effected had to be inserted on the policy itself. This was later amended by the Insurance Companies Act 1974 which allowed the categorisation of people by class or other description.

Marine Insurance Act 1788

By 1788 it was illegal to issue policies on British ships and goods laden on them and other insurances except ships, goods and merchandises, where no insurable interest existed. The loophole appeared to be policies effected on goods unconnected with a ship. The Act of 1788 remedied the position and insisted on insurable interest for policies on any ship or "any goods, merchandises, effects or other property whatsoever". The Act also required the name of one person interested or concerned to be inserted on the policy document.

The legislation up to this date had been restricted to insurance contracts and the Gaming Act 1845 was therefore introduced to render all contracts of gambling or wagering null and void. One effect of this as far as insurers were concerned was that insurance contracts where no insurable interest existed were rendered null and void as such contracts were nothing more than wagers.

Marine Insurance Act 1906

This Act repealed the 1745 Act and those parts of the 1788 Act relating to marine insurance. The Act codified these previous statutes and declared void any marine insurance contract where no insurable interest existed at the time of any loss. The Act is also interesting as it defines insurable interest in the following terms: "in particular a person is interested in a marine adventure where he stands in a legal or equitable relation to the adventure or to any insurable property at risk therein, in consequence of which he may benefit by the safety or due arrival of insurable property, or may be prejudiced by its loss, or by damage thereto, or by the detention thereof, or may incur liability in respect thereof".

Marine Insurance (Gambling Policies) Act 1909

Although gaming or wagering contracts were unenforceable nothing had been done to make them illegal until the passing of the 1909 Act. By its terms it was a criminal offence to effect a marine policy where no insurable interest existed or where there was no bona fide expectation of there being an interest.

Insurable interest required by statute

The aggregate effect of the legislation shown above is that by 1906 insurable interest had become an intrinsic feature of every valid policy of insurance.

Application of insurable interest to the main forms of insurance

It is not sufficient simply to be able to define the principle and discuss its development. What is of greater value is to understand its application to the everyday transaction of insurance. Here we will look at three of the more common forms of insurance—life assurance, property insurance and liability insurances—from which the general nature of the application of insurable interest may be understood.

Life assurance

Nowadays everyone has unlimited insurable interest in their own life and, theoretically, is entitled to effect a policy for any sum assured. In practice the cost of the policy often limits a person's ability to insure his or her own life. In addition to having insurable interest in one's own life, a person also has an interest in the life of his or her spouse. In this way wives can effect policies on the lives of their husbands and vice versa. This idea of mutual insurable interest is founded in common law but statutory authority for a wife to assure her own life was provided by the Married Women's Property Act 1882.

Apart from husband and wives a blood relationship does not imply an automatic insurable interest, the only exception to this being in the case of industrial life assurance where a person may assure the life of a parent, step-parent or grandparent up to an amount of £30 as provided by the Industrial Assurance and Friendly Societies Act 1948 and the Amendment Act 1958. This cover is really for funeral costs.

In line with our definition of insurable interest, certain people can insure the life of another person to whom they bear a relationship, recognised at law, to the extent of a possible financial loss. Accordingly partners can insure each other's lives up to the limit of their financial involvement as they would stand to lose on the death of any one of them. In the same way a creditor stands to lose money if a debtor dies before repaying the loan and therefore has insurable interest to the extent of the loan plus interest.

Property insurances

Insurable interest is perhaps most easily identified in property insurances. It normally arises out of ownership where the insured is the owner of the subject matter of insurance as in the case of a houseowner insuring his house, a sportsman insuring his golf clubs or a shopkeeper insuring his stock. There are, however, cases involving legal relationships and financial interests other than full ownership and some of these are given as follows:

Part or joint owners. A person having a partial interest in some property is entitled to insure to the full value of that property rather than just to the extent of his actual interest. This does not mean that he will benefit in any way should the property be destroyed completely as he is looked upon as a trustee for the other owner or owners. When he receives any claim money that exceeds his own financial interest he does so as an agent for the others and holds such money in trust for them.

Mortgagees and mortgagors. The involvement of mortgages is most common in the area of house purchase and involves a building society, the mortgagee, and the purchaser, the mortgagor. Both parties have insurable interest, the purchaser as owner of the house and the building society as a creditor. The interest of the mortgagee is limited to the extent of the loan. The normal practice in house purchase is for the building society to insist on the house being insured as a term of the mortgage contract.

Executors and trustees. We have already commented on the fact that executors and trustees often have a need to effect insurance on property they assume control over. They are legally responsible for the property under their charge and this gives rise to their insurable interest in it.

Bailees. A bailee is a person legally holding the goods of another either for payment or gratuitously. Pawnbrokers, launderers, and watch repairers are examples of bailees and each has a responsibility to take reasonable care of the goods and to look after them as if they were his own.

Agents. Where a principal has insurable interest his agent can effect insurance on his behalf.

Husband and wife. Each spouse has an insurable interest in the property of the other in much the same way as they have mutual insurable interest in each other's lives.

Liability insurance
A person has insurable interest to the extent of any potential legal liability he may incur by way of damages and other costs. It is not possible to pre-determine what the extent of that interest is as we do not know in what way and how often we may incur a liability. It could be said that the extent of a person's interest in liability insurance is without limit. In fact, as we saw in Chapters Two and Seven, policies are designed, with the exception of employers' liability, to provide cover up to a specified amount for any one event but either without limit in any one year for entirely separate incidents, or with an aggregate limit per annum arising out of all events.

When insurable interest must exist
In marine insurance, as we saw above, insurable interest need only exist at the time of any loss. This therefore protects merchants who may assume an interest in cargo, for example during a voyage, and may have

it included on a floating policy. In life assurance the rule is the reverse. Insurable interest needs to exist when the policy is effected, not necessarily at the time of claim. This principle was set down in the case of *Dalby* v. *The India and London Life Assurance Company* (1854) which reversed a judgement in *Godsall* v. *Boldero* (1807) that had held insurable interest need only exist at the time of claim.

For all other insurances, insurable interest must be present both at the time of effecting the policy and when any claim is made. The practical operation of certain covers, e.g. holiday insurance, has meant that policies are sometimes issued to commence at some future date.

Common features of insurable interest

In addition to any specific comments already made on the application of the doctrine to classes of insurance there are certain common features of insurable interest that are worthy of note.

Insurers' insurable interest. Insurers by accepting risks acquire an insurable interest themselves which of course entitles them to reinsure.

Enforceable at law. The mere expectation of acquiring insurable interest in the future, however certain that expectation is, may not be enough to create insurable interest. The case of *Lucena* v. *Craufurd* (1806) Provided an illustration of this point: "... suppose the case of the heir-at-law of a man who has an estate worth £20,000 a year, who is ninety years of age, upon his deathbed intestate, and incapable from incurable lunacy of making a will, there is no man who will deny that such an heir-at-law has a moral certainty of succeeding to the estate, yet the law will not allow that he has any interest, or anything more than a mere expectation".

Two exceptions to the general rule should be mentioned:

(*a*) A legal right depending upon an expectancy will result in insurable interest. In the case of *Cook* v. *Field* (1850) there was an agreement to sell an expectancy under a will for £2,000 and to repay the purchase money if the expectation was not realised. The purchaser was held to have an insurable interest in the life of the vendor of the expectancy.

(*b*) Expectancy founded on legal rights may create insurable interest. Perhaps the most common example of this is loss of profits insurance. A person or firm has no legal right to expect profits from the sale of goods or ownership of property but where they have insurable interest in the goods (*Barclay* v. *Cousins* (1802)) then they also have an insurable interest in the profits that they may expect if the goods or buildings are not damaged.

Equitable interest. Equitable interest may arise in a number of ways. For example where a formal mortgage deed has not been drawn up the lender will have an equitable interest in the property; such an equitable interest is enough to create insurable interest.

Possession. Lawful possession of property normally supports insurable interest provided that such possession is accompanied by responsibility.

Interest need not be specified. It is not necessary to state in a policy the precise nature of the insurable interest. In life assurance it is, however, necessary under the Life Assurance Act 1774 to mention by name the person who is to benefit from the assurance. However, the Insurance Companies Amendment Act 1973 permits unnamed persons to benefit, provided they fall within a certain class or description stated in the policy. It must be possible at any given time to establish the identity of any person who is entitled to benefit under a policy.

Criminal acts. A person cannot recover under a policy in respect of his own criminal acts (*Beresford* v. *Royal Insurance* (1938)) although it is quite in order to arrange insurance to meet the *civil* consequences of some breach of the criminal code. This happens regularly when drivers are found guilty of some road traffic offence and at the same time receive indemnity from insurers for damage to their own or another's property. No insurance is available in respect of any fine.

Financial valuation. It is generally said that insurable interest must be a pecuniary interest, but the difficulties with that proviso are clear when considering an interest in one's own life or the life of a spouse. The case of *Simcock* v. *Scottish Imperial* (1902) provided a more practical rule in the words "it must be in a reasonable sense capable of valuation in money". What can be said is that any value attaching to property through sentiment or pride does not give rise to insurable interest.

Statutory creation and modification of insurable interest
Statutes creating insurable interest
In addition to the ways in which insurable interest arises, shown above, it has also been created by statute in certain situations.

(*a*) *Settled Land Act 1925.* This Act gave insurable interest to tenants of property falling within the scope of the act.

(*b*) *Married Women's Property Act 1882.* This Act provided married women with an insurable interest in their own lives. It also entitled a woman to effect a policy on the life of her husband for her own benefit.

(*c*) *Repair of Benefice Buildings Measure 1972.* Diocesan Boards of Finance of the Church of England were obliged by this measure to insure any property for which they were responsible.

(*d*) *Industrial Assurance and Friendly Society Act 1948.* As we saw under "Life insurance" above, this act creates a limited form of insurable interest.

Statutes modifying insurable interest

We have seen already how certain people such as bailees, repairers, and so on may acquire insurable interest on the property of others held by them for which they are responsible. Over the years the liability of certain of these people was considered to be too onerous and statutes were passed to modify their liability. When the responsibility was modified it followed that the insurable interest was correspondingly reduced and it is for this reason that we are interested in these modifying statutes at this stage. One practical point worth bearing in mind is that while the statutes modified liability in certain instances, in others they left a full liability with the person who was originally liable. As a result the practical position relating to insurable interest may be unaltered.

(*a*) *Carriers Act 1830.* A common carrier is exempted from liability for certain valuable articles of greater value than £10 each, except where the value of the item has been declared and any extra charge paid.

(*b*) *Carriage of Goods by Sea Act 1971.* Liability of the carrier in this case is limited to 10,000 gold francs per package or unit, or 30 gold francs per kilo gross weight of the goods lost or damaged, whichever is the greater.

(*c*) *Hotel Proprietors Act 1956.* Where people have booked sleeping accommodation at an hotel and provided the hotelier displays a copy of the Schedule to the Act in a prominent position, his liability for loss of or damage to the property of guests is limited to £50 any one article and £100 any one guest. These limits do not apply where the loss or damage was brought about by the negligence of the proprietor or his staff, or in the case of goods deposited or offered for safe keeping.

(*d*) *Trustee Act 1925.* Trustees can effect fire insurance on trust property up to three-quarters of the value, paying the premium out of trust income. This Act does not alter the fact that in his own right the trustee can insure the property for its full value.

Assignment

We have noted already that it is the interest of a person in the subject matter of insurance that is insured by a policy. Any assignment or transfer of that policy from one person to another will cause problems as the new holder of the policy may not have the same insurable interest. Assignment of a policy, often referred to as transfer of rights, can be carried out but in the case of *personal contracts* the prior consent of the insurer is required.

The term *personal contracts* refers to the fact that the insurance company were influenced by the confidence they had in the insured and his ability to care for the subject matter of insurance. Fire and accident policies are considered *personal contracts* while life and marine policies are not.

The law relating to assignment is too complex for the scope of this book; we will therefore consider the assignment of personal contracts, life policies and marine policies.

Assignment of personal contracts. In general, assignment will be valid only with the consent of the insurers, as they will want to satisfy themselves as to the qualities of the new insured. The consent to assignment of the policy really constitutes a fresh contract and for this reason is often termed *novation.*

Assignment of life policies. Life policies are freely assignable as they are looked upon as being reversionary interests in view of the fact that the enjoyment of the rights in the policy are deferred. Three points arise in connection with assignment of life policies:

(*a*) it must be for consideration,

(*b*) the assignee need not have insurable interest in the life assured, and

(*c*) notice of the assignment should be given to the assurer.

The last point, although not compulsory, is advisable as it will give the assignee the right to sue in his own name under the policy according to the Policies of Assurance Act 1867.

Assignment of marine policies. Marine policies are freely assignable to anyone who may acquire an insurable interest in the subject matter of the insurance. In practice notice is usually required when assignment of hull insurances is being carried out. This is a reasonable safeguard to underwriters in view of the *personal* type nature of the contract, since the shipowner can influence the likelihood of loss to the hull, through the standard of management.

Assignment of policy proceeds

So far we have concentrated on assignment of rights under a policy as that is what is normally meant when assignment is mentioned. Another, less complex, form of assignment is where the proceeds of a policy are assigned—as in the case of a house-owner assigning the proceeds of the household insurance policy to a roof repairer. There is generally no objection to assignment of policy proceeds in this way as the insured is still in a contractual relationship with the insurers and must comply with all conditions and terms of the policy. All that is done is that the insurer is directed to make any claim money payable to some person other than the insured. Insurers can protect themselves when making such payment by asking the person receiving the money to sign a form discharging the insurer from any further liability.

The Married Women's Property Act 1882, the Married Women's Policies of Assurance (Scotland) Act 1880 and the Friendly Societies Act 1955 allow for *nominations* under life policies. This involves the assured in nominating a person to whom the policy proceeds should be paid and really constitutes assignment of the proceeds of the policy.

UTMOST GOOD FAITH

Most commercial contracts are subject to the doctrine of *caveat emptor* (let the buyer beware). These contracts are subject to the Sale of Goods Act 1893, the Misrepresentation Act 1967, The Supply of Goods (Implied Terms) Act 1973 and the Unfair Contract Terms Act 1977 but basically it is the responsibility of each party to the contract to ensure that they make a good or reasonable bargain. In most such contracts each party can examine the item or service which is the subject matter. So long as one does not mislead the other party and answers questions truthfully there is no question of the other party avoiding the contract. There is no need to disclose information which is not asked for.

However, when it comes to arranging insurance contracts, while the proposer can examine a specimen of the policy before accepting its terms, the insurer is at a disadvantage as he cannot examine all aspects of the proposed insurance which are material to him. Only the proposer knows, or should know, all the relevant facts about the risk being proposed. The underwriter can have a survey carried out but he must rely on information given by the insured in order to assess those aspects of the risk which are not apparent at the time of a survey.

In order to make the situation more equitable the law imposes a duty of *uberrima fides* or "utmost good faith" on the parties to an insurance contract. The contract is deemed to be one of faith or trust and most contracts of a fiduciary nature are subject to the same doctrine. This was summed up by Scrutton L.J. as follows: "As the underwriter knows nothing and the man who comes to him to ask him to insure knows everything, it is the duty of the assured . . . to make a full disclosure to the underwriter without being asked of all the material circumstances. This is expressed by saying it is a contract of the utmost good faith" (*Rozanes* v. *Bowen* (1928)).

Reciprocal duty. The duty of full disclosure rests on the underwriters also (*Carter* v. *Boehm* (1766)) and they must not withhold information from the proposer which leads him into a less favourable contract.

Material fact

The current legal definition of a material fact is contained in the Marine Insurance Act 1906, s. 18(2) in these words: "Every circumstance is material which would influence the judgement of a prudent insurer in fixing the premium or determining whether he will take the risk". This statement has been reaffirmed in the Road Traffic Act 1972 and in *Larbert* v. *C.I.S.* (1975) in similar terms. At the present time it is immaterial whether the proposer regards the matter as material or indeed, whether the individual insurer regards a fact as material, the test being the view of a prudent or reasonable underwriter. This long established legal rule is the subject of strong criticism today, and it is probable that the law will be changed (*see* "Modern developments" *below).*

Facts requiring disclosure
It is for the courts to decide if necessary whether or not a fact would be material to a prudent underwriter, but examples can be given of circumstances which are likely to be regarded as material:

(*a*) *Fire insurance:* the form of construction of the building and the nature of its use.

(*b*) *Theft insurance:* nature of stock and its value.

(*c*) *Motor insurance:* the fact that a vehicle will be driven regularly by someone other than the insured.

(*d*) *Marine insurance:* in cargo insurance, the fact that a particular consignment will be carried on deck.

(*e*) *Life assurance, personal accident insurance:* previous medical history.

(*f*) *In all classes of insurance:* previous loss experience and all facts which the proposer could be reasonably expected to know, e.g. a landlord should know the nature of occupancy of his property by a tenant.

Facts which need not be disclosed
It was stated earlier that everything is material which could influence the terms offered. It follows that in addition to the detrimental facts outlined in the previous paragraph, there could be facts which improve the risk and if the proposer does not disclose these facts he is not putting the underwriter at a disadvantage. There are other circumstances when the insurer may be assumed to be in possession of the full facts. Facts, even if material, need not be disclosed if coming within the following headings:

(*a*) *Facts of law:* everyone is deemed to know the law.

(*b*) *Facts which an insurer is deemed to know:* facts of common knowledge such as the strife in Northern Ireland or the usual or normal processes within a particular trade.

(*c*) *Facts which lessen the risk:* the existence of an alarm system in a theft risk or sprinklers in a fire risk.

(d) *Facts about which the insurer has been put on enquiry:* the most common example is where the proposer had referred the insurer to the claims record under a previous policy or with a previous insurer and he does not follow up this line of enquiry. The insurer will be regarded as having waived his right to the full information.

(e) *Facts which the insurer's survey should have noted:* material facts which are clearly visible, or which any reasonable surveyor would enquire about. On the other hand the proposer is not permitted to conceal material matters from the surveyor.

(f) *Facts covered by policy conditions:* a fact which it is superfluous to disclose by reason of any expressed or implied warranty, e.g. that burglar alarms are regularly maintained.

(g) *Facts which the proposer does not know:* one cannot be expected to disclose what is not known, but if it should have been within the proposer's knowledge there will be a duty to disclose it.

(h) *Facts (convictions) which are "spent" under the Rehabilitation of Offenders Act 1974.*

Duration of the duty of disclosure

At common law. The duty at common law starts at the commencement of negotiations for a contract and terminates when the contract is formed, i.e. when there is offer and acceptance. During the currency of the contract the duty is one of good faith, not of utmost good faith, in that at common law there is no need to disclose changes while the contract is running.

Contractual duty. Sometimes the conditions of a policy extend the common law position by requiring full disclosure during the currency of the contract, and giving the insurer the right to refuse to underwrite the change.

Position at renewal. The duty of disclosure at the time of renewal depends on the type of contract, for example:

(a) *Long-term business:* in these types of assurance (life endowment and permanent health) the assurer is obliged to accept the renewal premium if the assured wishes to continue the contract and there is no duty of disclosure operating at renewal.

(b) *Other business:* in other cases renewal requires the assent or agreement of the insurer and in such cases the original duty of disclosure is revived. The facts as applying at the time of negotiating the renewal must be disclosed (*Pim* v. *Reid* (1843)).

Alterations to the contract. If during the currency of the contract it is necessary to alter the terms of it, for example to increase the sum insured or alter the description of property insured, then there is a duty to disclose all material facts relating to the alteration.

Disclosure and the intermediary

It will be worthwhile to re-read the section on "The role of the intermediary" in Chapter Five at this point. Any intermediary negotiating on behalf of his principal is required to disclose any material facts within his principal's knowledge and also those facts which he has discovered in the course of his agency work. Similarly the knowledge of an agent will be imputed to his principal. An insurance company could not avoid liability on the grounds of non-disclosure if the material facts had been known to an employee but withheld from the underwriter. The actions of an agent may determine whether he is an agent of the insured or of the insurer at a particular time (*see* the *Newsholme Brothers* case, p. 84).

Representations and warranties

Representations

Written or oral statements made during the negotiations for a contract are termed "representations". Some of these statements will be about material facts and others not so. Those which are material must be substantially true or true to the best knowledge or belief of the proposer.

Warranties

In ordinary commercial contracts a warranty is a promise, subsidiary to the main contract, a breach of which would leave the aggrieved party with the right to sue for damages only. Warranties in insurance contracts on the other hand are fundamental conditions to the contract and a breach allows the aggrieved party to repudiate the contract. Their use and nature were discussed in Chapter Seven under "Warranties".

Implied warranty. In marine insurance there is an implied warranty or undertaking that the vessel is seaworthy.

Express warranties. The most common warranties are those written into the contract as described in Chapter Seven.

Comparison of representations and warranties

Representations	*Warranties*
(*a*) need only be substantially correct;	(*a*) must be strictly and literally complied with;
(*b*) a breach (misrepresentation) must be material to allow repudiation;	(*b*) any breach gives the right to repudiate;

Representations	*Warranties*
(*c*) do not normally appear on the policy.	(*c*) are written into the policy except for implied warranties. (There is no legal requirement to do this directly as the proposer may be asked to sign a warranty on the proposal form and the policy states the proposal is the basis of the contract.)

Breaches of utmost good faith

Breaches of utmost good faith may be classified as (*a*) innocent or accidental, and (*b*) deliberate or fraudulent.

    (*a*) *Innocent breaches:*
        (*i*) Non-disclosure—where information is withheld by accident.
        (*ii*) Innocent misrepresentation—where wrong information is given in the belief that is is true.
    (*b*) *Fraudulent breaches:*
        (*i*) Concealment—wilful withholding of information.
        (*ii*) Fraudulent misrepresentation—where wrong information is given deliberately or recklessly without caring whether it is true or false.

Remedies for breach of utmost good faith
The aggrieved party has the following options:

    (*a*) to avoid the contract by either (*i*) repudiating the contract *ab initio* or (*ii*) avoiding liability for an individual claim;
    (*b*) to sue for damages in addition to (*a*) if concealment or fraudulent misrepresentation is involved;
    (*c*) to waive his rights to (*a*) and/or (*b*) and allow the contract to carry on unhindered.

The aggrieved party must exercise his option within a reasonable time of discovery of the breach, or it will assumed that he has decided to waive his rights.

Breaches of utmost good faith under policies required by statute
Motor policies required by statute attempt to ensure that funds are available to meet the injury claims of third parties. The relevant statute prohibits the insurers from avoiding liability in the event of certain breaches of utmost good faith. Insurers do, however, endorse their policies to the effect that amounts paid in claims which would not have been paid, in the absence of statutory limitations, may be recovered

from the insured. The practical difficulties of recovering from an insured are so great that often insurers do not enforce this right.

Modern developments in the law of disclosure

Over twenty years ago doubts were cast on the fairness of the right of insurers to avoid liability because of non-disclosure. In 1957 a Law Reform Committee recommended that "for the purposes of any contract of insurance, no fact should be deemed material unless it would have been considered material by a reasonable *insured*", but that recommendation never reached the statute books.

The Unfair Contract Terms Act 1977

This Act requires that the terms and conditions contained in a contract are reasonable and outlaws many small-print exceptions. The Act does not apply to insurance contracts, and this concession was allowed on condition that the insurance industry issue "Statements of Insurance Practice".

Statements of Insurance Practice

In 1977 two Statements were issued, one relating to non-life business and the other to long-term business.

Non-life business. The voluntary undertaking relates to policyholders resident in the UK and insured in their private capacity only and covers proposal forms, claims and renewals. A summary of the more salient points is given below. The declaration at the foot of the proposal form should be restricted to the proposer's knowledge and belief; within the declaration or prominently displayed on the proposal, there should be a notice drawing the insured's attention to the consequences of non-disclosure and explaining the nature of a material fact; matters which insurers have found generally to be material must be the subject of specific questions. With regard to claims the insurers will not unreasonably repudiate liability (except in the case of fraud, deception or negligence) on the grounds of misrepresentation or non-disclosure where knowledge of the fact would not have affected the underwriting of the risk materially, nor on grounds of breach of warranty where the breach was unconnected with the loss. Renewal notices should warn the insured of the duty of disclosure and of changes which have occurred since inception or since last renewal.

Long-term business. The undertaking in respect of proposal forms and claims is in similar terms to those applying to non-life business, but in particular the insurers will not repudiate a claim in respect of non-disclosure or misrepresentation of a matter outside the knowledge of the proposer.

The Law Commission Report No. 104
This report was issued in October 1980, and once again recommendations were made regarding the duty of disclosure and warranties.

The Commission wished to see some of the points dealt with in the voluntary Statements of Insurance Practice enforced by statute. The main recommendations encompassed the following points:

Material facts. Facts should be disclosed if they would influence the prudent underwriter, *and,* they are facts which a reasonable applicant would know, should know, or would have made reasonable enquiries about, *and* are facts which a reasonable man in the position of the proposer would disclose.

Proposal forms. The insured's duty of disclosure should be restricted to answering to the best of his or her knowledge and belief. The form should contain warnings of the consequences of not giving accurate information, and the insured should be given a copy of the completed form.

Warranties. Insurers should not be able to avoid liability for a breach of warranty if the breach was not material to the loss.

Basis of contract clauses. Policies sometimes state that the proposal form is the basis of the contract. It is recommended that such undertakings be ineffective with regard to past or present facts.

At this time the recommendations have not been enacted, but since the consumer lobby is much stronger than in 1957 there is a strong possibility that changes in the law will come in the mid-1980s.

The exact wording of questions on proposal forms will be much more important if the recommendations are adopted, and the Commission feel that the *contra proferentem* rule should apply to the construction of proposal forms as well as policy forms (*see* Chapter Six). With regard to warranties, the warranty should be material to the risk and to the loss. In order to shorten proposal forms, certain companies have few questions on their forms, but ask if there are any facts which would influence the underwriter. The commission recommends that such questions should have no effect.

Conclusion
It can be seen that the law with regard to insurance disclosures is about to undergo some change. It is highly unlikely that the recommendations will receive the same fate as those in 1957. In the last two decades, a substantial amount of legislation has been put onto the statute books to protect the individual, and there seems to be no reason why insurance contracts should continue to be more or less exempt from the change in social feeling. If changes are adopted in the near future, the law on

disclosure is unlikely to remain unchanged for any considerable time, as the EEC are also considering the law in this area with a view to standardising it within the member countries. The EEC proposals differ substantially from those of the Law Commission and in due course the requirements of the EEC may prevail.

PROXIMATE CAUSE

Every loss is the effect of some cause, and as insurance policies either cover a limited type of loss, e.g. the standard fire policy, or cover many types of loss, but subject to various exceptions, e.g. an all-risks policy, then it is necessary to examine the cause of the loss in detail. Sometimes there is a single cause of loss, but frequently there is a chain of causation, or several causes may operate concurrently, and in these circumstances it may require considerable thought to decide whether the loss is within the scope of the policy or not. The doctrine which covers such deliberations is the doctrine of proximate cause.

Definition of proximate cause
The standard legal case on the topic is that of *Pawsey* v. *Scottish Union and National* (1907) where the doctrine was defined as follows: "Proximate cause means the active, efficient cause that sets in motion a train of events which brings about a result, without the intervention of any force started and working actively from a new and independent source".

The word "proximate" has the same meaning as near or nearest, and we are concerned with the nearest effective cause, which may not be the nearest or most recent cause in time. In general, causation is to be understood by the man in the street and by applying common-sense standards. For example, explosion is to be determined by its everyday meaning and not as an extremely rapid fire, as a chemist might view it.

Rules for the application of the proximate cause
(a) *The risk insured against must actually take place.* The fear of losing goods by an insured peril is not loss by that peril (*Moore* v. *Evans* (1918)).

(b) *Further damage to the subject matter due to attempts to minimise a loss already taking place is covered.* Therefore water damage from sprinklers or firemen's hoses is covered (*Johnston* v. *West of Scotland Insurance* (1928)).

(c) *"Novas actus interveniens"*, i.e. a new act intervening. We have seen in the definition from the *Pawsey* case that the intervention of a new act is outwith the doctrine. Thus if during a fire onlookers cause damage to surrounding property, the cause of such damage is the misdemeanours of the crowd and not the fire (*Marsden* v. *City & County Assurance Co.* (1865)).

(*d*) *"Last straw" cases.* In instances where the original peril has meant that loss was more or less inevitable, the original peril will be the proximate cause even though the last straw comes from another source (*Leyland Shipping Co. Ltd.* v. *Norwich Union* (1916); *Johnston* v. *West of Scotland* (1928)).

Nature of perils relevant to proximate cause
Perils which must be considered can come under three headings:

    (*a*) *Insured perils:* those named in the policy as insured.
    (*b*) *Excluded perils:* those named in the policy as not insured.
    (*c*) *Other perils:* those which are not mentioned at all.

If we denote these as I, E, and O respectively for ease of discussion, it can be said that all three can appear anywhere in a chain of events, the initial, the final, or any of the intermediate stages. In most insurance policies there are perils which are stated to be insured (I); others which are excluded (E) even if caused by I; some Is will only be covered if not caused by an E, and Os may cause an I or an E or be the result of either of them.

The standard fire policy is a good vehicle for explaining proximate cause and if we can look at excerpts from the operative clause and one of the conditions we can then illustrate its operation in various situations.

Excerpt from standard fire policy:

1. Operative clause.
    (*a*) "Fire (whether resulting from explosion or otherwise) not occasioned by . . .
        (*i*) its own spontaneous fermentation
        (*ii*) Earthquake . . . riot . . . war.
    (*b*) Lightning"
2. Condition 3.
    (*a*) "This policy does not cover explosion (whether the explosion be caused by fire or otherwise) except as stated on the face of the policy". (On the face of the policy only explosion of domestic gas or boilers is covered.)

Single cause
    EXAMPLE 1.

If storm blows a building down there is no claim as storm is not mentioned in the standard fire policy.

O ————→ O

EXAMPLE 2.

Lightning damages a chimney, so there is a valid claim.

I————→ O (collapse)

EXAMPLE 3.

Civil riot leads to a fire which causes damage. No valid claim.

E ————→ I (fire) ————→ no cover

Concurrent causes

This situation occurs where two or more causes act simultaneously without causation from one to the other. This does not happen very often but it is possible as in the case of a house being damaged by a storm, and during that storm a fire starting from a totally independent cause.

(*a*) If the effects can be separated only the loss from the insured peril is covered.

  ⎰ O (storm) ————→ O   (roof damage) ————→ not covered.
  ⎱ O (electrical fault) ————→ I (fire) ————→ I covered.

(*b*) If effects cannot be separated, both losses are covered.

  ⎰ O ————→ OI ————→ covered.
  ⎱ O ⟋

If instead of storm damage which is not mentioned in the policy there had been an excluded peril, e.g. explosion damage (other than domestic gas or boiler) independent of the fire damage, the position would have been:

(*c*) ⎰ E ————→ ————→ not covered   results
    ⎱ O ————→ I ————→ covered   separable

(*d*) Where effects cannot be separated there is no claim.

  ⎰ E ————→ E I ————→ no claim
  ⎱ O ⟋

Chain of causes

Far more common than the single or concurrent causes is the chain of events. An example occurred when a severe gale struck Glasgow a decade or so ago. Certain premises were insured by a standard fire policy which does not mention storm either as insured or as excluded. The hurricane blew down a timber building, breaking the electrical wiring which short-circuited, causing a fire. Other property was damaged by smoke and water. Using the symbols as before the result is:

$$\text{O (storm)} \to \text{O} \left\{ \begin{array}{l} \text{electrical} \\ \text{fault} \end{array} \right\} \longrightarrow \text{I} \quad \text{(fire)} \begin{array}{c} \nearrow \\ \searrow \end{array} \left\{ \begin{array}{l} \text{smoke damage} \\ \text{water damage} \end{array} \right. \begin{array}{l} \text{O} \\ \text{O} \end{array}$$

All damage from and including the fire damage was covered but not the damage caused by the storm or the electrical fault itself.

Practical examples

An examination of cases which have been decided in the courts is perhaps the best way to gain an understanding of proximate cause.

Gaskarth v. *Law Union (1872)*. A fire left a wall standing but in a weakened condition. Several days later, a gale caused the collapse of the wall onto other property. It was decided that the fire was not the proximate cause. It is sometimes quoted as stating that the gale was the proximate cause, but the crucial factor was the delay of several days during which no steps were taken to shore up the weakened wall. The chain had been broken:

$$\text{I (fire)} \to \text{I (damaged wall)/O (delay)/O (storm)} \to \left\{ \begin{array}{l} \text{further} \\ \text{damage} \end{array} \right.$$

Roth v. *South Easthope Farmers Mutual (1918)*. Lightning damaged a building and almost immediately afterwards storm blew it down. It was held that lightning was the proximate cause:

$$\text{I} \to \text{O} \to \text{loss}$$

In this second case there was not time to take remedial action and the danger created by the fire was still operating.

Walker v. *London & Provincial Insce. Co. (1888)*. A fire policy excluded arson. A fire was started in the premises next door by an arsonist and spread to the insured's premises. It was held that there was no claim as the proximate cause was an excepted peril.

$$\begin{array}{ll} \text{E} & \text{I} \end{array}$$
$$\text{(arson fire next door)} \to \text{(fire at insured's premises)}.$$

Leyland Shipping v. *Norwich Union (1916) (see "last straw" cases above)*. A marine policy excluded war risks. In time of war a ship was torpedoed and badly damaged. It managed to get to a port and repair

work was started but had to be stopped when a storm blew up. The
harbour-master ordered the ship out of port in case she sank and
blocked the harbour. Outside the harbour she met bad weather which
normally she would have survived, but in this case she sank. The
proximate cause of loss was war risks—the torpedo. The ship was in
danger of sinking from the moment she was torpedoed and as repairs
had not been completed that danger was always present.

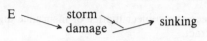

E —————→ storm damage ————→ sinking

To summarise, when an insured peril operates loss caused by it and all
losses directly flowing from other events created by the insured peril,
e.g. smoke or water damage, are covered unless:

(*a*) The insured peril was directly caused by an excepted peril;

(*b*) there is a break in the chain of events after the insured peril, when
cover will cease with the break;

(*c*) the policy wording modifies the basic principle.

In trying to establish whether there is an unbroken chain of events or
not, one starts at the original cause and asks what would *naturally*
happen next and having answered that, asks oneself the question again
and so on. If one reaches the final result there has been an unbroken
chain.

Modification of the principle by the policy wording

It was seen under "Nature of perils" above that most explosions are
excluded from the cover under the standard fire policy; therefore if an
acetylene gas bottle exploded and caused a fire it should be excluded
too, but the operative clause states "fire (whether caused by explosion
or otherwise)". The policy wording is overruling the principle so that
although the explosion damage is excluded, the fire damage is covered.
Similarly if fire causes an explosion the fire damage is covered but not
the explosion damage because Condition 3 excluded explosion even if
caused by fire.

The exact wording used must be examined closely to determine
whether or not the doctrine is amended. A fifth example illustrates this
point.

Coxe v. *Employers' Liability Ass. Corpn. (1916).* An army officer
had a personal accident policy excluding death directly or *indirectly*
due to war. In war time he was walking along a railway line to inspect
sentries when he was killed by a train. The proximate cause of his
death was *accident* but indirectly he was on the line because of the

war and the policy did not cover his death. War was only the remote cause but the use of the words "or indirectly" made it highly relevant.

SELF-ASSESSMENT QUESTIONS

Attempt the following questions and then refer to the appropriate paragraph to check your answer.

1. Distinguish between the subject matter of insurance and subject matter of the contract.
2. What are the four essential features of insurable interest?
3. Did the Life Assurance Act 1774 apply only to life assurance?
4. Does a parent have insurable interest in the life of his son?
5. Is insurable interest necessary when the claim occurs?
6. Is nomination in a life policy the same as assignment of rights?
7. In what way does the duty of disclosure in insurance contracts differ from that in other commercial contracts?
8. What is a material fact?
9. Which facts do not require disclosure?
10. What is the duration of the duty of utmost good faith?
11. Distinguish between representations and warranties.
12. What forms can breaches of utmost good faith take, and what are the possible remedies in each case?
13. Define proximate cause.
14. State the details and conclusions in the following cases:
    (1) *Gaskarth* v. *Law Union* (1876);
    (2) *Leyland Shipping* v. *Norwich Union* (1916);
    (3) *Johnston* v. *West of Scotland* (1928).
15. How may policy wordings override the doctrine of proximate cause?

CHAPTER NINE

Basic Doctrines II

CHAPTER OBJECTIVES

After studying this chapter you should be able to:
* explain the principle of indemnity and its corollaries, subrogation and contribution;
* indicate their applications to the main classes of insurance.

INDEMNITY

Rationale and definition

Indemnity was once said by Lord Justice Brett in the case of *Castellain* v. *Preston* (1883) to be the "controlling principle in insurance law". As can be expected, a principle that is so central to the operation of insurance has not existed without there being a fair deal of dispute over its exact application. As we progress through our study is it possible to come to the conclusion that indemnity is responsible for many of the day-to-day disputes and disagreements with which insurance personnel are confronted.

The essence of the problem that the principle of indemnity addresses is best posed in question form: What is a person to receive when the insured-against event occurs? Take a factory owner who bought a machine for £5,000 five years ago. It is completely destroyed by fire and will cost £15,000 to replace. How much should he receive? Bear this problem in mind and we will hope to answer it later.

Definition

One dictionary definition of the word "indemnity" is "the protection or security against damage or loss or security against legal responsibility". The idea of security and protection fits in well with our knowledge of the development of insurance and gives some hint as to the meaning of indemnity. We could look upon indemnity as a mechanism by which insurers provide financial compensation in an attempt to place the insured in the same pecuniary position after the loss as he enjoyed immediately before it.

A further quotation from *Castellain* v. *Preston* (1883) is worthy of note as it emphasises the important position indemnity plays in insurance.

The very foundation, in my opinion, of every rule which has been applied to insurance law is this, namely, that the contract of insurance contained in a marine or fire policy is a contract of indemnity and of indemnity only . . . and if ever a proposition is brought forward which is at variance with it, that is to say, which either will prevent the assured from obtaining a full indemnity or which gives the assured more than a full indemnity, that proposition must certainly be wrong.

Relationship with insurable interest

There is a link between indemnity and insurable interest as it is the insured's interest in the subject matter of insurance that is in fact insured. In the event of any claim the payment made to an insured cannot therefore exceed the extent of his interest, and as we will see later there are often cases where insureds receive less than the value of their interest (*see* "Limitations on the payment of indemnity" *below*).

As with insurable interest, the principle of indemnity relies heavily on financial evaluation and this leads us to consider the position of those policies where such valuation is difficult. In life assurance and personal accident insurance there generally is an unlimited interest and in these cases indemnity is not possible. Another way of phrasing this same point is to say that life and personal accident policies are not contracts of indemnity as the value of a person's life or limb cannot be measured by money. There can be exceptions to this general rule where specific policies are effected in the case, for example, of a personal accident policy effected by an employer on his staff where the policy is intended to provide him with any amount he would have to pay in wages to a sick employee.

Methods of providing indemnity

The popular belief among many is that insurers will do all within their power to do as little and pay as little as possible in the event of a claim. The time of a claim is always a difficult one for many reasons not least of which is the fact that the insured is, invariably, suffering from some degree of shock and it would not be to the advantage of insurers to exacerbate this already difficult problem by being "awkward". The option as to how indemnity is to be provided is normally given to the insurers by the wording of the policy but insurers will normally comply with insured's requests as far as method of settlement is concerned as long as it does not unnecessarily increase costs. The following represent the main methods by which indemnity is provided.

Cash payments. This is the most common method of settlement and involves the insurer simply in making a cash payment, representing indemnity, to the insured. In liability insurance cash payments are always made, although in the majority of cases the insured is bypassed and the money paid to the third party direct.

Repair. Insurers make extensive use of repair as a method of providing indemnity in motor insurance, where garages are authorised to carry out repair work on damaged vehicles.

Replacement. The most common example of replacement is found in glass insurance where windows, etc. are replaced on behalf of insurers by glazing firms. Insurers normally enjoy a discount in view of the vast amount of work paid for by them. Replacement can also be used in special cases where it seems the most acceptable method to both parties. An example may be where a diamond is lost from a ring containing two stones. The best method of settlement may be for the insurers to direct the insured to a jeweller in order that an attempt could be made at matching the existing diamond by replacing the lost one. An increasing use of replacement is being made by some motor insurers where a nearly-new car is destroyed and replaced by a similar model. The insured obtains a new car and the insurers enjoy the benefit of any discount. This is a deviation from the strict interpretation of indemnity in view of the wear and tear suffered by the destroyed vehicle, but not deducted from the new one.

Reinstatement. This much over-used word will be used in two different contexts in this chapter in addition to its use in Chapter Seven. As a method of providing indemnity it refers to property insurance and the case where an insurer undertakes to restore or rebuild a building damaged by fire. As with repair and replacement, difficulties can arise if an insured is not entirely satisfied with the final work of reinstatement but use of policy monies for reinstatement can be compulsory under the terms of the Fires Prevention (Metropolis) Act 1774. Under this statute any interested party can insist on reinstatement.

How the sum payable is assessed

A claim under a policy of indemnity has been said, in the case of *Jabbour* v. *Custodian of Israeli Absentee Property* (1954), to be a claim for unliquidated damages. This means that the exact amount of the compensation is not known before the loss occurs. This is clear in the case of damage to property, liability insurances and other non-life policies but in the case of life assurance and personal accident policies the amount of money to be paid in the event of a claim is, generally, a liquidated amount, i.e. is known before the claim takes place.

The method by which indemnity is to be measured depends on the nature of the insurance involved and the main forms are considered below.

Property insurance

The general rule is that the measure of indemnity in respect of the loss of any property is determined not by its cost (*Aubrey Film Productions* v.

Graham (1960)) but by its value at the date (*Hercules Insurance* v. *Hunter* (1836)) and at the place of the loss (*Rice* v. *Baxendale* (1861)). If the value has increased during the currency of the policy the assured is therefore entitled to an indemnity on the basis of the increased value (*Wilson* v. *Scottish Insurance Corporation* (1920)) subject of course to policy limits such as sum insured or average. In assessing the amount of this value no allowance is to be made for loss of prospective profits or other consequential loss (*Wright* v. *Pole* (1934)) or for mere sentimental value (*Re Egmont's Trusts* (1908)).

These are very general guidelines and examples of their application in specific cases follow.

Buildings and machinery. In the event of total destruction indemnity will be based on the estimated repair or replacement costs with a deduction for wear and tear and, if applicable, betterment. If we return to the example given in the second paragraph of this chapter we see that the insured is faced with the total destruction of his machine purchased five years ago for £5,000. Our definition of indemnity, above, suggests that the insured is to be placed in the same financial position that he enjoyed immediately prior to the loss. Bearing in mind the general rules and case law shown above, indemnity is not determined by cost, so we can rule out the £5,000, but is is determined by its value at the date of the loss. This value is crucial to the settlement and where the insured can go into the market and restore himself to his original position the market value of the property will, on the face of it, be the basis of the amount recoverable.

Returning to our example we know that the replacement value of the machine at the time of the loss was £15,000. Subject to any limitations on the amount payable, this would be our base figure. The insured, however, cannot receive £15,000 as he would then be in a better position after the loss than he was before because he would be able to buy a brand-new machine. What must be taken into account is wear and tear. He had had five years use of the machine which may be half, one-third, one-quarter, or whatever, of its expected life. Let us say that all parties agree the expected life of the machine to be ten years. In that case the insured would be entitled to £7,500 subject to the limits mentioned above.

Note: One practical consideration in today's world of fast-moving technological advances is that the same machine that was purchased five years ago is no longer manufactured, although an improved version is available. In such a case a compromise would have to be reached with the insured, possibly on guidance from the manufacturer, as to the value of any new features on the machine.

In partial loss cases the cost of repairs is normally the measure of indemnity but again some consideration must be given to wear and tear and betterment.

Stock. When stock is destroyed we must be careful to bear in mind that prospective profit from the sale of the stock is not to be included in any settlement. The insurers are concerned only with the property itself and will base their settlement on the purchase price of the stock, at the time of the loss, to the retailer or wholesaler who has suffered the loss and will add to that figure an amount in respect of any handling costs incurred to the date of the destruction or loss. In the case of farmers the marketing expenses saved by the loss of the stock must be deducted from any settlement.

Household goods. The same considerations as with buildings and machinery apply but one added problem is often encountered where the insured attaches some sentimental value to a damaged or lost article. Sentiment is a subjective value, not capable of any objective measurement, and if the insured is to be placed in the same *financial* position after a loss then such a settlement must exclude any thoughts of sentiment.

As indemnity is based on the cost of replacing at the time of loss, subject to wear and tear deductions, it is essential to review sums insured annually to keep abreast of price increases, for these increases certainly exceed depreciation especially in the case of durables such as kitchen equipment, suites and the like.

Pecuniary insurances

In guarantee policies the measure of indemnity is comparatively easy to ascertain as it will amount to the actual financial loss suffered by the insured as a result, say, of the dishonesty of a cashier. In consequential loss insurance it is a little more difficult to establish indemnity but it is one of the very few policies where the steps to be taken in the event of a claim are detailed. With the help of the insured's accountants it is necessary to try and establish what profit the firm would have made if the fire had not occurred and compare this to what actually was made, the difference providing the basis of indemnity.

Liability insurance

Indemnity is most easily established in liability insurance. It is the amount of any court award or negotiated out-of-court settlement plus costs and expenses arising in connection with the claim.

Life assurance and personal accident insurance

These contracts are not generally regarded as being contracts of indemnity but that is not to imply that care is not exercised in settling claims. Rather than indemnity being exercised at the time of a claim, as is the case in indemnity contracts, caution is exercised when the contract is effected in life and personal accident business. In life assurance the amount by which a person may be insured is limited by his own ability to meet premiums and in personal accident policies offering weekly benefits it is limited to an amount that will not provide an unreasonably high benefit in relation to a person's normal earnings.

Salvage

Where property is destroyed to the extent that it has ceased to exist then the problem of salvage obviously does not arise. Where property is not damaged to this extent but remains in a deteriorated or damaged condition the question of salvage does arise. Take a shoe-shop where stock has been damaged extensively by fire. The shoes are not destroyed but are damaged by smoke; they are in other words in a deteriorated condition. The insured can only claim the value of the loss to him, which would probably amount to having the shoes cleaned, unless he agrees to hand over the shoes that are left to the insurers. *If the insured does not agree to treat the property as wholly destroyed he cannot insist on having it wholly made good to him.* This was established as long ago as 1873 in the case of *Rankin* v. *Potter* and on the basis of that conclusion property insurers are entitled to any materials left following damage where they have agreed to pay a loss in full. In the shoe-shop example the insurers would take over the salvaged shoes, or more likely a loss adjuster would do so on their behalf, and sell them to reduce their overall outlay.

Abandonment

This only arises in marine insurance, in the form of the *constructive total loss*. According to the Marine Insurance Act 1906, s. 60, there is a constructive total loss where "the assured is deprived of the possession of his ship or goods by a peril insured against, and (*a*) it is unlikely that he can recover the ship or goods, as the case may be, or (*b*) the cost of recovering the ship or goods, as the case may be, would exceed their value when recovered". The definition imagines a situation where the property is not destroyed completely, as in the case of a total loss, but it is as good as lost as far as the insured is concerned, as for example in the case of a ship which runs aground on a sandbank and cannot be refloated. The insured abandons her to underwriters and the claim is dealt with as if it was a loss with the vessel becoming the property of the insurers. Abandonment is not permitted in fire and non-fire damage to property policies.

Value added tax

There is one important consideration which we have not taken into account. The price of most goods and services provided in this country is subject to a value added tax (VAT), the current rate being 15 per cent. The repair or replacement values which we have discussed will include, for most trades and commodities, 15 per cent tax. For the private individual, very small traders (turnover under £17,500 per annum), and a few businesses which are "exempt rated", the indemnity value arrived at will be the correct one. In the case of the vast majority of commercial and industrial organisations which submit claims, the full cost of repairs will give them more than indemnity. The reason is that they can offset or recover any VAT paid by them against the VAT which they charge on the sale of their own product, and only pay Customs and Excise the difference. In settling claims in such cases we must deduct the amount of VAT on the repair costs, since they will be able to recover that amount from Customs and Excise. If VAT was not deducted they would be paid the 15 per cent twice, once by the insurer and once by Customs and Excise.

Limitations on the payment of indemnity

All that has been said so far on measuring and providing indemnity is qualified by certain limiting factors, which will now be dealt with. These factors are not intended to make an insured suffer in any sense following upon a loss and indeed need not prejudice the insured's position at all if policies are arranged properly.

The sum insured

The limit of an insurer's liability is the sum insured. This is essential to the operation of insurance and is easy to overlook when handling a complex claim. The insured cannot receive more than the sum insured even where indemnity is a higher figure—as will arise where an insured has not updated his policy. The exception to the general rule is in liability insurance where insurers agree to meet certain costs and expenses over and above the limit of indemnity. (As we saw in Chapters Two and Seven, liability policies use limit of indemnity as opposed to sum insured but what we have said in relation to the insurer's maximum liability applies equally to limits of indemnity and sums insured.)

Average

The operation of average was discussed in Chapter Seven and by referring back you will see how it can limit the amount payable. Where there is under-insurance the insurers are receiving a premium only for a proportion of the entire value at risk and any settlement will take this into account using the formula:

$$\frac{\text{Sum insured}}{\text{full value}} \times \text{loss.}$$

When average operates to reduce the amount payable the insured really receives less than indemnity but, theoretically, he is being considered his own insurer for a portion of the risk and in a sense should "indemnify himself ", for the balance not received from the insurers.

> *Note:* One interesting development in recent times has been the move towards applying some form of average on household insurance policies, a class of business traditionally free of average. Household insurers have been experiencing large losses partly due to under-insurance and the application of average is considered, by some, to be an answer to this.

Excess

The excess has also been looked at before and where it applies to reduce the amount paid it certainly results in the insured receiving less than indemnity. Again theoretically, we could say the insured is his own insurer for the first £50, £75 or for whatever value the excess represents. Apart from those cases where excesses are imposed for some underwriting reason the insured will normally have the benefit of a reduction in premium as a result of the application of the excess.

The operation of a *franchise,* distinguishable from an excess as when the amount of the franchise is exceeded the whole loss is paid including the value of the franchise, will also limit the amount payable. The franchise is not very common and its use is restricted really to those cases where there has been a history of small claims.

Limits

Many policies limit the amount to be paid for certain events by the wording of the contract itself. The household contents policy normally has a wording that says "no one curio picture work of art . . . is deemed to be of greater value than 5 per cent of the sum insured on contents". In the event of a work of art valued at £750 being destroyed in a household fire where the contents sum insured was £6,000, subject to the insured not having intimated to the insurers that he wished the item covered, he would receive less than indemnity, i.e. £300.

A different wording to the one used above is where insurers say, "in the event of a loss not more than £100 will be paid in respect of any one item". In this case they acknowledge that items in excess of £100 may exist but that any claim payment would be limited to that figure.

In either case it is for the insured and his advisers to ensure that he is adquately protected.

Deductibles

One aspect of commercial insurance that has increased over recent years, and shows signs of increasing, is the use of deductibles. A deductible is the name given to a very large excess. An industrial insured may consider that they have the resources to meet fire claims up to £50,000 in any one period of insurance and be confident in their own ability to prevent fires. They may approach an insurer and receive a discount from the premium. In the event of a claim they will not receive indemnity as they have decided that they will settle for less than indemnity in order to obtain the savings in premium

Property being sold

One final factor that may limit indemnity, or what some consider should be indemnity, it the knowledge that the insured was endeavouring to sell the property at the time of the destruction. A recent case, *Leppard* v. *Excess Insurance Company Ltd.* (1979), revolved around this point. In 1974 Mr. Leppard took out a household policy on the structure of an empty cottage he owned, and was trying to sell. The proposal form contained the declaration that the sum insured represented "not less than the full value (the full value is the amount which it would cost to replace the property in its existing form should it be totally destroyed)". In October 1975 the cottage was completely destroyed by fire and Mr Leppard claimed that indemnity was the sum insured, which by the declaration was the full value of £14,000. The insurers contended that he was only entitled to recover his *actual loss* which in this case was the market value £4,500 less the site value of £1,500. At the county court the judge disagreed with the insurers but on appeal it was found that since the insured was ready and willing to sell the cottage at the time of the fire his *actual loss* was £4,500, the selling price, less the site value of £1,500.

This judgement enforces what we have said about indemnity and did not really limit the operation of indemnity as the insured was put back in the same financial position he enjoyed before the loss.

Modification of the principle by the policy wording

Marine insurance

In marine insurance it has long been the practice for a commercial indemnity, rather than the strict insurance indemnity described above, to be given. This form of indemnity, in the words of the Marine Insurance Act 1906, attempts to indemnify the insured "in manner and to the extent thereby agreed". In fact for hull and cargo policies *agreed value* policies are arranged with the value being agreed between the insured and insurer. The hull value allows for a fair commercial value to the shipowner and the cargo value allows the merchant to include his profit as well as the cost of the goods, hence the earlier reference to a *commercial indemnity*.

Reinstatement

Here is the second use of the word reinstatement. Its use here refers to the method used in arriving at the amount payable in respect of a claim under a property policy covering buildings or machinery. The insured can request that his policy be subject to the "reinstatement memorandum" and as a result the method of settlement will provide the insured with an amount that has been calculated without deduction of wear, tear and depreciation. The insurers agree to pay the full cost of the reinstatement at the time of reinstatement. This would mean that the settlement includes indemnity *plus* wear, tear and depreciation *plus* the effects of inflation between date of loss and eventual date of reinstatement. This is a very valuable cover as one can imagine, and in the case of our example at the beginning of the chapter would have given the insured the full £15,000 subject to any other limitations not applying. The problems posed by betterment still exist, and insurers protect themselves by saying that they will reinstate to the position when new but that the property must not end up in a better or more extensive condition than when new. An element of contribution would be required from the insured in the event of the unavailability of exactly the same machine with available machines being better.

Reinstatement cover is not paid for by an increase in the rate percent but is paid for by the fact that the sum insured has to represent not less than the cost of reinstatement at the time of reinstatement. Sums insured will therefore be substantially higher on reinstatement policies than on indemnity contracts and consequently the premium paid will also be greater.

Household contents insurance "new for old"

This is similar to the reinstatement covers described above and is found in different forms on different policies. At its basic level the insurer agrees to pay for reinstatement of contents if they are destroyed within a certain number of years of their purchase, say three or five, without deduction of wear and tear. In a fuller form "new for old" cover is offered without time limit for all contents with the exception of items such as clothing and linen.

Agreed additional costs

In property insurance the insured often incurs additional costs as a result of a fire or other damage. He may have to remove debris from the site, comply with public authority requirements when rebuilding and incur architects' and surveyors' fees. These costs can be included within the insured's cover and any payments relating to them will amount to more than strict indemnity.

Note: In special cases additional costs are met where indemnity would not be "fair". An example of this arises where raw tobacco or cotton is destroyed and in view of the limited supply of these commodities the price will rise. This means that the insured would have to pay the inflated price to replace his lost goods, the loss of which caused the price increase. Insurers in such cases have agreed to compensate the insured and this constitutes more than strict indemnity.

Valued policies

We have already discussed valued policies in relation to marine insurance but they are also used in certain other special cases. Where there is an article of particular value, a piece of jewellery or work of art the insured could obtain the advice of an expert on value and arrange a policy where the amount to be paid in the event of a total loss is determined at inception. It can be argued that valued policies do not modify indemnity as in the case of partial losses indemnity still operates and in the event of a total loss all that has been done is to agree the measure of indemnity before the loss.

SUBROGATION

Two doctrines follow on from indemnity and are said to be corollaries of it; they are subrogation and contribution. Without these two concepts the operation of indemnity would not be possible.

Rationale and definition

The principle of indemnity, already studied, states that a man is to be placed in the same financial position after a loss as he enjoyed immediately before the loss. A major effect of this principle is therefore that a man cannot recover more than his loss: he cannot profit from the happening of an insured event. There can be circumstances where a man may receive indemnity from an insurer, then find he also has some common law or statutory right to reimbursement from some other source. A simple example may be the case of a painter using a blow-lamp, where as a result of his negligence the house burns down. The house owner can raise an action against the painter and also has a right to claim an indemnity from his insurers. In a case like this it is certainly unjust to let the innocent party recover twice, once from the negligent painter and again from his insurers.

Definitions

Subrogation is the right of one person to stand in the place of another and avail himself of all the rights and remedies of that other, whether already enforced or not. As far back as 1882 in the case of *Burnand* v. *Rodocanachi* the principle was put forward that an insurer, having indemnified a person, was entitled to receive back from the insured anything he may receive from any other source.

It is important to note here that we are not saying that the insured cannot recover from a source in addition to his own insurers. What is being said is that, should he succeed in so doing, the money he acquires is not his but is held in trust for his insurer who has already provided an indemnity.

Corollary of indemnity

Subrogation only applies where the contract is one of indemnity, and our authority for saying this is found in the case of *Castellain* v. *Preston* (1883)—"that doctrine [subrogation] does not arise upon any terms of the contract of insurance; it is only another proposition which has been adopted for the purpose of carrying out the fundamental rule, i.e. indemnity which I [the judge] have mentioned, and it is a doctrine in favour of the underwriters or insurers in order to prevent the assured from recovering more than a full indemnity; it has been adopted solely for that reason".

Preston was in the course of selling his house to Rayner when it was destroyed by fire. He recovered from his insurers, Liverpool & London and Globe, and subsequently when the conveyance of the property was completed, which was prior to repairs being carried out, also received the full purchase price from Rayner. The insurers sued in the name of their chairman, Castellain, and were successful in recovering their outlay.

It follows therefore that life contracts, for example, are not subject to the doctrine of subrogation as they are not contracts of indemnity and if death was caused, say, by the negligence of another person then the deceased's representatives may be able to recover from that source in addition to the policy moneys.

Limit on what insurers can recover

Due to the link between subrogation and contribution an insurer is not entitled to recover more than he has paid out. In other words the insurers must not make any profit for exercising their subrogation rights. An insured may receive a full indemnity but may later succeed in recovering more than the claim payment from the third party. This situation arose in a case known as *Yorkshire Insurance Co. Ltd.* v. *Nisbet Shipping Co. Ltd.* (1961) where settlement had been made at £72,000 by the insurers but due to the lapse of time between the claim payment and the recovery from the third party and due to the fact that the pound sterling had been devalued in the interval, the insured actually recovered £127,000. It was held that the insurers were entitled only to £72,000.

In this case Lord Justice Diplock confirmed what had earlier been stated in the case of *Glen Line* v. *Attorney General* (1930) that "subrogation will only give the insurer rights up to 20s. [100p] in the £ on what he had paid", by saying, "the simple principle which I apply is that the insurer cannot recover under the doctrine of subrogation . . . anything more than he had paid".

Subrogation rights limited to indemnity

This was recently amplified in *Scottish Union & National Isurance* v. *Davis* (1970) where insurers had paid £409 for repairs and attempted to subrogate as the insured had received £350 from another source. In fact the repairs were useless and no satisfaction note had been signed by the insured; the judge held the insurers were not entitled to recover, saying "so far as the assured was concerned, they [the insurers] might have thrown £409 in bank notes into the Thames". This strengthens the link between subrogration and indemnity: insurers can only subrogate to the extent that they have provided indemnity.

Where the insured has been considered his own insurer for part of the risk, as in the case of an excess or the application of average, he is entitled to retain an amount equal to that share of the risk out of any money recovered.

Note: The payment of an ex gratia payment would not entitle the insurer to subrogation rights if an insured also received from some other source as such payments are not looked upon as being indemnity.

Ways in which subrogation may arise

Subrogation rights arise in four ways. The rationale behind subrogation is the support of indemnity in order that a person should not recover from two or more sources in the event of him having been already indemnified by an insurer. What we will consider here are the ways in which insurers may find that they have the right to recover their outlays from some party other than the insured.

Right arising out of tort

The briefest definition of "tort" is that it is a civil wrong. Tort forms part of the common law of England and incorporates negligence, nuisance, trespass, defamation and other legal wrongs. Where the insured has sustained some damage, lost rights or incurred a liability due to the tortious actions of some other person then his insurer, having indemnified him for his loss, is entitled to take action to recover the outlay from the tortfeasor or wrongdoer involved.

This arises in very many ways. A motorist driving negligently may strike and damage buildings, tradesmen may negligently leave factory doors open allowing thieves to steal some stock, a painter might drop ladders onto a machine and it could be damaged and production lost. In each of these cases the person suffering the loss could have had a policy to indemnify him—a household buildings policy, a theft policy and an engineering extraneous damage policy. In addition to the indemnity from his insurers the insured would have a right, in tort, against the motorist, tradesman and painter. The insurers assume these rights and attempt to recover their outlays from the appropriate party. Any action the insurers take is in the name of the insured and his permission would be sought if legal action was found to be necessary.

Another practical reason for seeking the insured's permission to take legal action is that he may well have an uninsured claim he wants to include. The law does not allow you to sue a person more than once arising out of the same event.

Right arising out of contract

One other part of the common law is contract. In relation to subrogation we are concerned with those cases (*a*) where a person has a contractual right to compensation regardless of fault and (*b*) where the custom of the trade to which the contract applies dictates that certain bailees are responsible, e.g. the hotel proprietor or common carrier. The insurers then assume the benefits of these rights.

Common examples of rights arising out of contract are found in many tenancy agreements where tenants agree to make good any damage to the property they occupy. Prudent property owners would also maintain a policy of insurance and in the event of damage to the property may find it easier to recover under it in the first instance. Where they do recover they are not also entitled to the compensation from the tennant (*Darrell* v. *Tibbitts* (1880)) and the insurers assume the rights to any money from that quarter.

Right arising out of statute

Under the Riot (Damages) Act 1886, where a person sustains damage mentioned in the Act and is indemnified, his insurers have a right *in their own name* to recover their outlays from the police authority.

The Railway Fires Act (1905) Amendment Act (1923) removed a defence normally enjoyed by the railways for damage by sparks and cinders, but only in respect of agricultural land or uncut crops to a value of £200, later voluntarily increased by British Rail to £400.

Rights arising out of the subject matter of insurance
Where an insured has been indemnified in the case of a total loss he
cannot also claim the salvage as this would give him more than
indemnity. It can be argued therefore that when insurers sell salvage, as
in the case of disposing of damaged cars, stock or machinery, they are
really exercising their subrogation rights in support of the principle of
indemnity.

When the right of subrogation arises

The common law right of subrogation does not arise until the insurers
have admitted the insured claim and paid it. This could, however, give
rise to some problems as the insurers would not have complete control
from the date of the loss and their eventual position could be prejudiced
by delay or other action on the insured's part.

To ensure their position is not prejudiced, insurers place a condition
on the policy giving themselves subrogation rights before the claim is
paid. The insurer cannot of course recover from the third party before
he has actually settled with his own insured but the express condition
allows the insurers to hold the third party liable pending indemnity
being granted to the insured person. The altering of the common law
position does not arise in marine insurance where in every case the
claim must be met before the underwriters have subrogation rights.

Irrespective of whether an express subrogation condition appears on
a policy or not, any action must be taken in the insured's name. The
only exception to this rule is the case of the Riot Damages Act when the
insurers can proceed in their own name. The rights which pass to the
insurers by virtue of subrogation are the rights which the insured has.
As the insurers could not maintain an action against the third party in
their own right, certain obligations are placed upon the insured; namely
to assist the insurers in enforcing claims and to do nothing that might
prejudice the insurer's chances of recovery.

It is worthwhile also to note that although subrogation is intended as
a back-up to the principle of indemnity it has one other useful side
effect and that is that in many cases if a man received indemnity from
his insurers he may decide not to proceed against some other person
who may be liable, say in negligence, to him. Subrogation has the effect
then of ensuring that these negligent persons are not "let off the hook"
simply because the insured was prudent enough to arrange insurance.

Modification in the operation of subrogation

In very many cases the exercising of subrogation rights by one insurer
involves him in claiming money back from another. In the case of a
motorist damaging property, the property insurer would be exercising
subrogation rights against the driver who in turn would pass that claim

on to his own motor insurers. As you can imagine, insurers would find themselves involved in correspondence for each such event and in view of the volume of business would probably also find that they were exercising subrogation rights against a company one day and paying out to that same company the next, when roles were reversed.

This situation is very noticeable in motor insurance and in consequence subrogation rights are waived by certain insurers, who have become parties to the "knock-for-knock" agreement. This is strictly an inter-company agreement and means simply that insurers will not exercise subrogation rights against each other for damage to their own insureds' vehicles.

Other agreements exist, for example one between motor insurers and property insurers who cover impact damage by motor vehicles, whereby the companies agree to contribute towards losses by pre-determined proportion. In employers' liability subrogation is waived where one employee causes the injury of another. In the absence of this rule we would have the unacceptable situation where insurers would be taking action against one employee on behalf of the insured, his employer. This rule is itself waived where there is some knowledge that the employees concerned are acting together to obtain some financial benefit from their employers.

These modifications are also discussed under "Claims settlements" in Chapter Seven.

CONTRIBUTION

We have already seen that a man may have a right to receive an indemnity from his insurance company and also from another party who is legally responsible for the financial effects of the incident which has taken place. This man may also have a right to recover his loss from two or more insurers with whom he has effected policies to cover this type of loss.

In the first instance the corollary of indemnity called "subrogation" operates allowing the insurers to take over the insured's rights against the third party, thus upholding indemnity and ensuring that legal wrongdoers do not receive benefit from another's policy.

In the second instance, the principle of indemnity prevents the insured from being more than fully indemnified by each of his insurers, and another corollary called "contribution" ensures that the insurers will share the loss as they have all received a premium for the risk. As far back as 1758 Lord Mansfield said "if the insured is to receive but one satisfaction, natural justice says that the several insurers shall all of them contribute, pro rata, to satisfy the loss against which they have all insured" (*Godin* v. *London Assurance*). There is no question here of the insurers exercising subrogation rights which must normally be raised in the insured's name, because they have the right to contribution in their own names in equity (*North British & Mercantille* v. *Liverpool & London & Globe* (1877)). Contribution applies only to contracts of indemnity so does not apply to life policies nor normally to personal accident policies.

Definition
Contribution is the right of an insurer to call upon others similarly, but not necessarily equally, liable to the same insured to share the cost of an indemnity payment.

When the right to contribution arises
At common law contribution will only apply where the following conditions are met:

(*a*) two or more policies of indemnity exist;
(*b*) the policies cover the same or a common interest;
(*c*) the policies cover the same or a common peril which gave rise to the loss;
(*d*) the policies cover the same or a common subject matter;
(*e*) each policy is liable for the loss.

The policies do not require to cover identical interests, perils, or subject matter so long as there is an overlap shared by them e.g.:

1.		B	
2.		B	C
3.	A	B	C

In these boxes A, B and C represent in each case interest, or peril or subject matter. Policy (1) would be in contribution with (2) and (3) in respect of any loss involving B and policy (2) would be in contribution with (3) for a loss involving C.

The same or common interest
The leading case in contribution is that of the *North British & Mercantile* v. *Liverpool & London & Globe* (1877), known as the "*King and Queen Granaries*" case. Merchants, Rodocanachi, had deposited grain at the granary owned by Barnett. The latter had a strict liability for the grain by the custom of his trade in London, and had insured it. The owner had insured it to cover his interest as owner. When the grain was damaged by fire the bailee's insurers paid and sought to recover from the owner's insurers. As the interests were different, one as bailee

and one as owner, the court held that contribution should not apply.

Where a policy is effected in joint interests, e.g. landlord and tenant, and the tenant has a policy in addition covering his interest alone, perhaps for building improvements, there would be contribution but only in respect of the amount of loss falling on the tenant.

When contribution operates
At common law
When an insured has more than one insurer, he can confine his claim to one of them if he so wishes. That insurer must meet the loss to the limit of his liability and at common law can only call for contribution from the other(s) after he has paid. This is still the position in marine policies, and it means that this unfortunate insurer has to lay out all of the money until such time as he makes a recovery. He also has the trouble of negotiating the method of sharing the loss. To overcome this difficulty most non-marine policies contain a "contribution condition".

By contractual condition
The condition contained in most policies states that the insurer is liable only for his "rateable proportion" of the loss. The insurer is liable for his share only, and the insured is left to make a claim against the other insurer if he wishes to be indemnified. It should be noted that the condition *does not require* the insured to claim from the other policies, although in practice he will elect to do so.

The basis of contribution
The application of contribution and loss apportionments will be studied in considerable depth by many readers in later years and it is sufficient for the purposes of this book to indicate in outline the basic methods of application.

Property policies (not subject to average)
In the case of policies which are not subject to average (*see* Chapter Seven) it is usual to determine the amount of contribution by each insurer in proportion to their sums insured in accordance with the formula.

$$\frac{\text{Sum insured by particular insurer}}{\text{Total of sums insured of all insurers}} \times \frac{\text{Loss}}{1} = \begin{array}{l}\text{Liability of}\\\text{particular}\\\text{insurer}\end{array}$$

Example
Company A insures house contents for £6,000
Company B insures them for   £4,000
The insured loses £1,000 in a fire ∴

$$\text{Office A would pay} \quad \frac{£6,000}{£10,000} \times \frac{£1,000}{1} = £600$$

$$\text{Office B would pay} \quad \frac{£4,000}{£10,000} \times \frac{£1,000}{1} = \frac{£400}{£1,000}$$

Other property policies

In the case of policies which are subject to average, or where an individual loss limit applies within a sum insured, one must use the "independent liability" method to calculate the payments. The "independent liability" is the amount which an insurer would be obliged to pay if it were the only or independent insurer.

As more policies become subject to average, and as terms limiting liability below the indemnity figure become more common, this method will become almost universal in use. Even at present, where contribution does arise, it is the most frequently used method.

The formula used is:

$$\frac{\text{Insurer's independent liability}}{\text{Total of all insurers' liabilities}} \times \frac{\text{Loss}}{1} = \frac{\text{Liability of}}{\text{individual insurer}}$$

Example 1

Property is insured with companies A and B for £2,000 and £1,000 respectively and the value of the property is £4,500. In the event of a loss of £450, with both policies being subject to average, the contribution is:

$$\text{A's liability} \quad \frac{£2,000}{£4,500} \times £450 = £200$$

$$\text{B's liability} \quad \frac{£1,000}{£4,500} \times £450 = \frac{£100}{£300}$$

Example 2

If the sum insured by A above had been £4,500 the other figures remaining unaltered the solution would be:

$$\text{A's liability} \quad \frac{£4,500}{£4,500} \times \frac{£450}{1} = £450$$

$$\text{B's liability} \quad \frac{£1,000}{£4,500} \times \frac{£450}{1} = \frac{£100}{£550}$$

Here the total of the independent liabilities comes to more than the loss, which is then shared in proportion to the independent liabilities

$$\therefore \quad \text{A pays} \quad \frac{£450}{£550} \times \frac{£450}{1} = £368.20$$

$$\text{B pays} \quad \frac{£100}{£550} \times \frac{£450}{1} = \underline{\underline{\begin{array}{r} £81.80 \\ \overline{£450.00} \end{array}}}$$

Liability policies. The independent liability method is always applied to liability policies where contribution is to be applied. This practice was given legal backing in the case of *Commercial Union Assoc.* v. *Hayden* (1977).

Modifications of the principle
Non-contribution clauses
Sometimes the equitable right to contribution is removed by a clause in one or both of the policies, e.g.:

> This policy shall not apply in respect of any claim where the insured is entitled to indemnity under any other insurance *except in respect of any excess beyond the amount which would have been payable under such other insurance had this insurance not been effected.*

Under this full clause the insured may have a claim under the policy containing it but only if the other policy does not pay indemnity, and then only for the balance of loss, i.e. there is not "rateable" sharing. Some clauses do not contain the words in italics, in which case the policy would not pay whether the insured had received an indemnity or not.

More specific insurance clauses
When a policy is issued covering a wide range of property, clauses similar to that shown above are sometimes inserted to prevent contribution between the wide range policy and any which might be more specific. For example, a fire policy on stock anywhere in the UK would not contribute with a marine policy covering a particular cargo consignment in a dock-side warehouse, nor a house contents policy in respect of a ring insured under an all risks policy.

Common law agreement
Many insurers are party to an agreement in relation to injuries suffered by employees being carried in the employer's vehicle in the course of

their employment. In these circumstances there could be a claim in law under the motor policy and the employer's liability policy. The market agreement states that such claims will be dealt with as employer's liability claims and there will be no contribution with the motor insurers.

Fire Offices' Committee rules
Under certain rules of the FOC (*see* Chapter Five) contribution may be applied in certain cases where it would not apply in common law, e.g. where interests are different as in the case of bailees and bailors or owners, subject to certain limits which would leave small losses on a non-contribution basis.

Different interests
In the absence of a market agreement like that mentioned in the preceding paragraph it is possible for a loss to be paid twice to different interested parties who are each entitled to be indemnified. This was the situation in the cases of *Scottish Amicable Heritable Securities* v. *Northern* (1883) and *Westminster Fire* v. *Glasgow Provident Investment Soc.* (1888).

A mill in Glasgow was the subject of two mortgages and was damaged in a fire. This damage reduced the value of the building and so injured the interest of each lender. In the first case the mortgagees sought payment for the estimated cost of repair and were paid. Instead of carrying out repairs, they used the money to reduce their loan, thus leaving the second mortgagees with a reduced security. In the second case, the mortgagees were held to be entitled to recover the cost of repairs, in order to be able to repair their security. Because of the different interests there was no contribution and the insurance market paid the loss twice.

This is a case for a joint reinstatement, but the election by an insurer to reinstate a building is fraught with legal difficulties.

Insured's rights
Subject to the "rateable proportion" clause referred to above, any contribution at common law or by market agreement must not interfere with nor delay the insured's right to be indemnified (subject to policy limits) by any insurer with whom he is insured.

SELF-ASSESSMENT QUESTIONS
Attempt the following questions and then refer to the appropriate paragraph to check your answer.

1. What is the link between indemnity and insurable interest?
2. How does replacement differ from repair as a method of providing indemnity?
3. Would you say a claim under indemnity was one for liquidated or unliquidated damages?
4. How would you assess indemnity on retail stock?
5. What is the limit of the insurer's liability under an indemnity policy?
6. When does reinstatement of the sum insured following a claim not apply?
7. Does a valued policy modify indemnity?
8. In what way does subrogation support indemnity?
9. What is the extent of an insurer's subrogation rights?
10. When subrogation arises out of tort in whose name would any action be taken?
11. How and why do insurers modify the common law right of subrogation?
12. What is the link between indemnity and contribution?
13. When does contribution arise?
14. How is the amount of contribution calculated?

CHAPTER TEN

Reinsurance

CHAPTER OBJECTIVES

After studying this chapter you should be able to:
* outline the reasons for reinsurance;
* describe the main methods of reinsurance, distinguishing between proportional and non-proportional reinsurance;
* indicate the application of reinsurance to the main classes of insurance business.

OBJECTS OF REINSURANCE

We have seen in Chapter Three that insurance is a mechanism whereby individuals or firms can, for a known premium, transfer the risk of losses of uncertain magnitude to an insurance company. By offering this service, an insurance company hopes to make a profit as a return on the capital invested in the business. As a result, the problems of uncertainty which faced the insured now confront the insurers and for several reasons they themselves may find it necessary to effect insurance, hence the term "reinsurance".

Terminology

Reinsurance. "Insuring again" is the literal meaning, and it entails insuring with someone else part (or all) of the risk which has been insured by a member of the public, i.e. insurance of insurance.

Ceding office. The insurers who have accepted a larger risk from the public than it is prudent for them to carry, and have "ceded" or given away the surplus to a reinsurer.

Reinsurer. One who accepts reinsurance from a ceding office or direct insurer.

Cession. The amount of insurance given or ceded to the reinsurer.

Treaty (or automatic reinsurance). An insurance contract arranged between the ceding office and reinsurer(s), whereby the reinsurer(s) will accept *automatically* without further negotiations such cessions as the ceding office wishes to place in the future. This agreement or treaty will be for a certain time period, say one year or three years, and will be subject to restrictions as to type of risk or values involved. Under the treaty, there may be one of several reinsurers sharing whatever is ceded in fixed proportions.

Retention. The amount of risk retained or kept for their own account by the ceding office. This would be the maximum net loss which the ceding insurer judged that it would be prudent to keep, bearing in mind how long they had been transacting that class of insurance, the financial status of their account in that class of business, the nature of the particular proposal being dealt with, and whether the maximum probable loss with respect to that proposal was equal to or less than the sum being proposed for insurance. When dealing with perils such as fire or explosion, it is not only the proposal in question which must be considered but also all other policies which could be affected by a single incident. The retention fixed by the underwriter would take into account all such potential liabilities.

Retrocession. This is the act of reinsuring what has been accepted under a reinsurance contract.

Purposes

The purposes of reinsurance could be said to be covered under the following headings.

Capacity. As the direct insurers can reinsure part of certain risks they can therefore accept more of the original risk. It could be that a particular insurer has calculated that he would not want to provide fire insurance cover for manufacturers of plastic goods where the sum insured was in excess of £100,000. Should he receive an inquiry from such a potential insured and the sum to be insured was, say, £400,000, he would be in a difficult position if it was not for reinsurance. With this available, however, he could accept the whole £400,000 in the knowledge that reinsurance exists for the £300,000 not retained by himself. The exact ways by which this is achieved are shown later in this chapter. The result is growth within the insurance market as a whole and added prestige to the individual insurer.

Stabilisation. Just as the insured has no knowledge of when a claim will occur or what it will cost, similarly the direct insurer also lacks this knowledge. The insurance company has a far greater experience of handling losses, and statistical techniques can assist the prediction of losses and their costs; nevertheless there is still considerable uncertainty. Reinsurance helps the direct insurer to stabilise their loss levels by removing some of the uncertainty. An insurer who has issued a public liability policy with an indemnity limit for any one occurrence of £250,000 has no idea when a claim may arise or what it will cost. Such an insurer may agree with a reinsurance company or companies that they (the direct insurer) will pay the first £50,000 of each claim, leaving the balance, whatever it may be, to be met by the reinsurer(s). In this way, the insurance company has reduced the possible fluctuation in claims costs and it should result in the company being able to produce more accurate budgets and reserves based on a more certain claims expenditure estimate.

Confidence. One of the advantages of insurance was shown to be the giving of confidence. In the knowledge that a large number of uncertainties has been removed, a manufacturer may be more willing to invest money in his business. In exactly the same way the existence of reinsurance gives confidence to an insurer and encourages expansion of that company's business. An example of this is found where an insurer wishes to offer insurance in an area in which he has had no previous dealings. With limited experience in the new area the insurer may be rather hesitant. The existence of reinsurance, however, removes many of the uncertainties and should make the insurer a little more confident. If the insurer was considering offering theft insurance for the first time he may not want to encounter a claims ratio greater than 70 per cent, i.e. when claims paid are compared to premiums received, the result should not be greater than 70 per cent. In the absence of reinsurance, there would be no guarantee of this. With reinsurance, the direct insurer may agree with a reinsurer or reinsurers that, if the ratio did go beyond the 70 per cent, they, the reinsurer(s), would pay the balance or part of it.

Catastrophe protection. If the worst possible state of affairs combined together to produce losses of catastrophic proportions, then the financial resources of a direct insurer would be seriously strained. Reinsurance acts as a cushion to protect insurers against this eventuality.

Spread of risk. Insurance has been shown to be a mechanism by which the impact of losses is spread. Reinsurance also serves this purpose—it is a mechanism by which direct insurers can spread their losses. The direct insurer may not want a concentration of liability in any one type of business, any one class of risk, any one geographical area or in any other classification. By organising reinsurance facilities correctly it can spread the potential impact of future losses.

FORMS OF REINSURANCE

There are two methods of classifying the forms which reinsurance may take, and each of these methods has the same two broad sub-divisions. Every form of cover will come under one sub-division of each method. First, a reinsurance contract can be described as either participating or non-participating. Secondly, the contract can be described as having been arranged in advance for use as and when required, i.e. a treaty contract, or be one which has to be negotiated individually as the risk arises, i.e. a facultative contract. This is illustrated in Fig. 8.

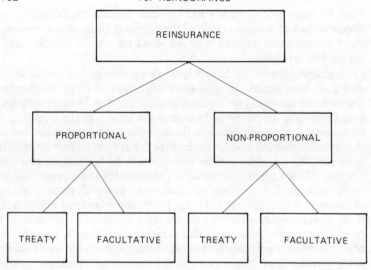

Fig. 8. *Forms of reinsurance contract.*

Participating or proportional reinsurances

Under these forms of reinsurance the amount retained and the amount ceded will represent certain proportions of the cover accepted by the ceding office, and the premium received by the ceding office will be shared in these same proportions. When a claim is intimated to the ceding office by their client, the claim payment will be shared by the ceding office and the reinsurers in the same proportions, irrespective of the size of the claim.

Line

The capacity of any participating reinsurance contract is measured in "lines", one line being equal to the ceding office's retention. Under treaty arrangements, the maximum acceptance limits of the treaty reinsurers will be stated in "lines". If a direct insurer had a five-line treaty, they could accept business from the public up to six times their retention, i.e. keep their retention (one line) and cede five lines to the reinsurance treaty.

Although the reinsurers receive a share of the full premium for the risk, they allow a commission to the ceding office to cover their procuration, survey and administrative expenses. This rate of commission will be considerably higher than the rate of commission paid by the ceding office to its intermediary, so that in addition to the main function of spreading the risk, there are income benefits to the ceding office when it places resinsurance. For example, if the sum insured under a policy was £100,000 and the company could retain 20 per cent and had a four-line treaty, the risk would be shared in this manner:

Retention	£20,000 = 1 line	= 20% in this case
Reinsurance treaty	£80,000 = 4 lines	= 80% in this case
	£100,000	

If a claim of £1,000 was paid under the policy, the ceding office would recover 80 per cent or £800 under its treaty leaving it a net liability of £200 (20 per cent).

It is likely that the treaty would not be underwritten by one reinsurer, but rather that several would be sharing the contract. Reinsurer A might underwrite 25 per cent of the reinsurance, B 20 per cent, C and D 15 per cent each, E and F 10 per cent each and G 5 per cent of the amounts ceded to the treaty. The claim would be shared by the insurers under their treaty in the following manner:

Reinsurance claims settlement

Division of amount ceded			Division of claim
A	25%	£20,000	£200
B	20%	£16,000	£160
C	15%	£12,000	£120
D	15%	£12,000	£120
E	10%	£8,000	£80
F	10%	£8,000	£80
G	5%	£4,000	£40
		£80,000	£800

The main types of proportional reinsurance are as follows:

Surplus treaty

The ceding office has a treaty arrangement whereby the subscribers to the treaty will accept any surplus risk over the retention of the ceding office. During negotiations the ceding office's maximum retention sum for each type of risk will have been specified, and certain types of risk may be excluded from the treaty, e.g. in fire insurance, plastics without protection from sprinklers and wood-working risks.

When a risk is proposed the ceding office has a free choice, within the limits mentioned above, of how much it will retain for its own account, and if the sum insured is less than its normal retention level for that class of risk, it need not reinsure at all, i.e. it will "retain all". The reinsurers are compelled to accept up to the the number of lines specified in the treaty if reinsurance is desired. Sometimes, in order to increase the underwriting capacity of the ceding office, it enters into a *second surplus treaty* whereby another group of reinsurers will write a certain number of lines in addition to those written under the first surplus treaty. The second treaty will not become involved in a risk until the ceding office has committed the first treaty to its full capacity.

Quota share treaty

This is similar to a surplus treaty except that the ceding office must reinsure such proportion of every risk as stated in the treaty. It cannot "retain all" of any risk, no matter how small the sum insured. With surplus treaty business, there may be a temptation for the direct underwriter to accept poorer class business and keep a low retention and/or to keep very high retentions on good risks. This would be to the detriment of the reinsurers especially when there is a large number of lines in the treaty. In quota share business, this freedom of choice is removed and the reinsurers are getting an equitable share of good and bad risks.

Quota share treaties are used where:

(*a*) a company has not been long in a particular market and its underwriting experience is unknown and yet it requires substantial reinsurance protection;

(*b*) a company's surplus treaty claims experience has been poor and this may be the only form of reinsurance cover available to it; and

(*c*) it is seen as a means of saving costs by way of earning higher commission rates than on surplus treaties and cutting the administrative time on making retention decisions.

Under both surplus and quota share treaties, it is usual for the reinsurers to be unaware of the individual risks which they are insuring. The treaties are "blind treaties" and the ceding office prepares an account periodically showing the proportion of premiums due to the reinsurers and the proportion of claims due from them.

Facultative

This is the earliest form of reinsurance cover, but is still used (*a*) where treaty capacity has been filled, (*b*) where the risk is outwith the terms of the treaty, and (*c*) for unusual risks. Each risk is reinsured separately and each party is completely free to decide whether to reinsure or not and whether to accept the reinsurance or not. The reinsurer has freedom of choice of how much of the risk to insure and at what commission rate. The ceding office must make a full disclosure of the material facts of the case (*see* Chapter Eight) and these facts would include the level of the ceding company's net retention and the rate of premium.

Facultative reinsurance is relatively expensive to purchase because of the increased costs of administration and the fact that the risks offered for facultative cover are likely to be heavier by way of extra hazards and/or will be of higher value. The main advantage of treaty business is that the ceding office can give immediate cover to the public, knowing that they have reinsurance cover from the moment they make a decision regarding the amount of their retention. Immediate decisions cannot be given, however, where the ceding office has to seek facultative cover.

Non-participating, non-proportional or excess reinsurance

In these forms of cover the ceding office and the reinsurers do not share each loss in fixed proportions, and may not share some losses at all. The ceding office will underwrite its retention as a form of first loss insurance, i.e. it will bear all losses up to a certain figure, and the reinsurers will deal with the balance of any loss above this figure, with usually an upper limit.

Excess of loss reinsurance

This is written on an individual risk basis, whereby the ceding office will pay for all of the first layer of each claim, say £50,000, and the reinsurers will pay the balance up to perhaps £250,000. If the direct or ceding office expects to incur losses above this level, it will require a second layer or excess of loss cover from, perhaps, £250,000 to £500,000.

If a claim was intimated for £300,000, the direct office would pay this figure and recover £200,000 from the first reinsurers and £50,000 from the second, leaving it with a net liability equal to its retention of £50,000. This form of cover can be arranged on a treaty basis, or facultatively as for proportional reinsurance. The amount of retention will vary according to the financial resources of the ceding office, the type of peril, e.g. fire or liability, and the nature of the risk being underwritten.

Catastrophe excess of loss

Even assuming that responsible underwriting has been undertaken in respect of proportional or non-proportional reinsurance arrangements for individual risks, there could still be an accumulation of net claims arising out of the one event whereby the financial stability of the company, at least for that year, could be threatened. Flood, storm, and earthquake are just three examples of perils which could create claims under many policies over a wide area, and the total amount of the net retention under each of the policies affected could come to a substantial figure.

A company may arrange excess of loss cover for amounts exceeding £100,000 or £250,000, for example, of their total net liability arising out of the one event. Sometimes they retain a percentage, say 10 per cent, of each layer of reinsurance as an incentive to cautious underwriting. A company would expect to have reinsurance claims under its catastrophe excess of loss cover very rarely as it is arranged by way of an emergency reserve. On the other hand, it would expect to have claims on its excess of loss covers on an individual risk basis, at least in the lower layers, from time to time.

Excess of loss ratio or stop loss reinsurance
This form of reinsurance differs from the rest in that it does not deal with individual risks or individual events, but is designed to prevent wide fluctuations of the net claims ratio of a particular account over one financial year compared with another.

For example, if the average ratio of net claims to net premium income in a company's fire account was 60 per cent over a period of years, they might wish to prevent the ratio going much above 70 per cent in any one year, and would arrange reinsurance accordingly. It is normal to require the ceding office to bear a share, say 10 per cent, of any layer of reinsurance. If the company bought reinsurance cover for 90 per cent (i.e. bearing 10 per cent itself) of any excess of claims ratio above 70 per cent up to 100 per cent, then in the event of claims amounting to £800,000 compared with premium income of £1,000,000, the result would be as follows:

Ceding office first 70%	£700,000 (balance £100,000)
Reinsurers 90% of balance	£ 90,000
Ceding office 10% of balance	£ 10,000
	£800,000

Their claims ratio would therefore be 71 per cent compared with 80 per cent without reinsurance. If claims had exceeded £1,000,000, the whole of the losses above £1,000,000 would have been borne by the ceding office. As claims ratios vary from year to year, there would always be a margin between the average ratio (60 per cent in this case) and the start of the reinsurance layer (70 per cent in this case). The reinsurance is intended to protect the company from an abnormal experience and not just the normal year-to-year fluctuations.

Premium calculation for non-proportional business can be extremely complex and is beyond the scope of this text. However, one of the main factors will be the "burning cost" or a comparison of the total cost of claims which would have fallen within each layer of excess cover in the past, compared with the premium income for the risk as a whole.

Reinsurance pools

Pools are sometimes arranged for exceptionally hazardous risks. The member companies may not retain any of the risks accepted in the direct market but reinsure 100 per cent into the pool. Each member then accepts a prearranged percentage of the business in the pool, sharing in the losses and profits in these proportions. Nuclear energy risks, certain aviation risks and, in life assurance, coronary and blood pressure cases are examples of risks handled in this way. Because of the wide spread of risk achieved by this method, cover can be provided for risks which would otherwise be uninsurable, or only accepted for extremely low sums insured.

APPLICATIONS OF REINSURANCE

Our knowledge and understanding of how reinsurance can be used to its best advantage is always increasing and it is not possible to state with absolute certainty what forms of reinsurance are best for particular classes of direct insurance business.

It is possible to give some guidance based upon the two divisions of reinsurance already described, i.e. proportional and non-proportional. As we saw, proportional reinsurances depended upon accepting a proportion of a risk, paying claims in the same proportion and charging a premium that was the same proportion of the direct insurer's premium. This is only possible where the extent of the risk is known beforehand, as in property insurances. In the case of liability business, for example, there is no reasonably foreseeable limit to the amount which may have to be paid and for such forms of direct insurance the non-proportional reinsurances are more appropriate.

Property

Proportional forms of reinsurance are most common in the property field as in most cases there is a fixed sum insured upon which a proportion can be calculated. Surplus and quota share treaties are used widely in the property market, with facultative catering for risks excepted by the reinsurers or for catastrophe cover. Excess of loss reinsurance is now becoming more common in the property field as a result of the American influence on the British market.

As we saw in Chapter Seven, several direct insurers may share a risk as co-insurers on a collective policy. The reinsurance facilities dealt with here are available to each of these co-insurers in respect of their individual sum insured under the collective policy.

Liability

Excess of loss reinsurance is used almost exclusively by liability insurers as it relies on the value of claims as opposed to a proportion of the risk. In addition to straightforward liability insurance, the excess of loss form of reinsurance can also be applied to the liability sections of other policies, e.g. motor.

Marine and aviation
Marine and aviation risks are really a combination of property and liability insurances and, for this reason, direct insurers must arrange reinsurances to suit such perils. Facultative reinsurance is still common in the marine market with quota share and excess of loss also being employed. The catastrophe element attached to marine and aviation risks must also be catered for and the pooling method of reinsurance, referred to above, can be used.

Life and personal accident
As might be expected, the reinsurance arrangements for life and personal accident contracts are slightly different from those in the non-life field. It is common to refer to "reassurance" for these long term contracts in line with the use of the term life "assurance".

For ordinary life assurance risks, reassurance may be arranged on a facultative or treaty basis. The difference between reassurance and reinsurance lies in the basis upon which reassurance is provided. Two options are available, "original terms" and "risk premium basis". In the former, the reassurer(s) divide the total premium and sum assured in a given proportion with the reassurer following all the terms and conditions of the direct office's policy. The 'risk premium basis' is a more complicated method but in essence the reassurer is involved only in the mortality risk and receives a very low premium at inception of a policy, as the chance of the assured dying is very low, and receives more of the premium as the years pass.

Particular reassurance pools are in existence for sub-standard lives such as those assureds with a history of diabetes, high blood-pressure or coronary heart disease.

SELF-ASSESSMENT QUESTIONS

Select the correct option or options under each of the questions shown below.

1. The purpose of reinsurance is to:
   (a) pass the risk of loss to the reinsurance market so that the ceding office avoids paying claims;
   (b) develop still further the doctrine that "the losses of the few shall be paid by the many".

    (c) help the insurance market to have confidence in meeting the challenge of the risks created by advances in technology;

    (d) give the public more confidence that their insurers will be able to pay their claims.

2. (a) In excess of loss reinsurance the reinsurers will pay a fixed percentage of each claim.

    (b) Surplus treaty reinsurance is fairer to the reinsurer than quota share.

    (c) If a ceding office's retention is £10,000 and it has a 5 line treaty it can accept £60,000 from the public.

    (d) Stop loss reinsurance is designed to stabilise the underwriting results of the company from year to year.

3. Surplus treaty can be used for: (a) fire insurance; (b) liability insurance; (c) third party motor insurance; (d) theft insurance.

National Insurance

HISTORICAL DEVELOPMENT

National Insurance is really outside the scope of activities of those engaged in commercial insurance but a knowledge of what is involved in the national scheme is important, not only for the purposes of examination, but also for the sake of completing and rounding off our knowledge of insurance protection.

Background

Almost all who will read this book will have spent their entire lives under the protection of some form of "welfare state". In these circumstances it is extremely difficult for us to cast our minds back to pre-welfare state days but such days did exist and they were very harsh. Many plays, books and films portray the lot of the unfortunates who found themselves unable to earn a living through ill health or just through lack of work. The Elizabethan Poor Law Act (1601) really marked the start of the state assuming some responsibility for social security and the responsibility for the relief of poverty was placed on the parish within which a person lived.

Although the eighteenth and nineteenth centuries saw the progression of the Poor Laws and the existence of workhouses, the coming of the industrial revolution and the consequent move towards towns made the position acute. Some employers did a little to help employees but the position was bleak, well described in many Dickens novels, especially for the underprivileged such as orphans, widows and the elderly.

State intervention

A Royal Commission on poor law and relief was established in 1905 and it recommended the separate treatment of sickness, unemployment and old age. A National Insurance Act was passed in 1911 introducing the three-fold method of payment involving employers, employees and the state. The Act provided for sickness and maternity benefits for manual and certain non-manual workers. The Act also introduced unemployment insurance. A number of amending statutes were passed in following years but the landmark came in 1942 with the publication of the Beveridge Report on Social Insurance and Allied Services. The government accepted the report in principle and an extended scheme of National Insurance began in August 1948.

NATIONAL INSURANCE TODAY

Britain's current system dates back to 1948 and the Beveridge Report and is operated by a number of local offices spread throughout the country.

Operation of the scheme

In general everyone in Britain pays National Insurance contributions if they are sixteen or over and employed with earnings above a minimum level or alternatively are self-employed. It is these contributions together with employers' payments and state contributions that pay for benefits. Rates of contributions do change and schedules are available from the Department of Health and Social Security but a rough guide as to the proportions each pay would be that employers pay, on average, twice what the employee pays.

Classes of contribution

Class 1 contributions. These are paid by employees and their employers. The contributions are calculated on gross pay and are collected through PAYE income tax arrangements. The contributions are earnings-related.

Class 2 contributions. Paid by self-employed people, normally by direct debit to a bank or by stamping a contribution card.

Class 3 contributions. These are voluntary and can be paid to enable a person to qualify for extra benefits, as shown on the schedule of benefits below.

Class 4 contributions. Paid by self-employed people when profits are over a specific level in any tax year.

The benefits available

The benefits shown below are paid out of the National Insurance Fund but entitlement depends, among other things, on the amount and class of contributions paid.

	Class 1	Classes 2 & 4	Class 3
Unemployment benefit	✓	✗	✗
Sickness and invalidity benefits	✓	✓	✗
Maternity allowance	✓	✓	✗
Maternity grant	✓	✓	✓
Widow's benefits	✓	✓	✓
Child's special allowance	✓	✓	✓
Death grant	✓	✓	✓
Retirement pension	✓	✓	✓

Unemployment benefit. Only class 1 (employees) contributions count towards this benefit and it is available to people who are out of work but fit and available for work should it be available. A basic rate is paid plus an amount for wife or adult dependent, an amount for each child and in certain cases an "earnings-related supplement".

Sickness and invalidity benefits. Sickness benefit is payable to people who can provide medical evidence of their inability to work. Benefits are paid in the same way as for unemployment benefit. Where someone has been in receipt of sickness benefit for more than twenty-eight weeks they go on to invalidity benefit.

Maternity allowance. Where a woman has paid, herself, full-rate contributions on earnings in the tax year related to her claim she is entitled to an allowance of a fixed amount for up to eighteen weeks.

Maternity grant. Every woman who has a baby is entitled to the one-off maternity grant, presently £25, where either she or her husband have been making contributions.

Widows' benefits. Widows' benefits are based on the late husband's contributions and take the form of a widow's allowance payable for the first six months of widowhood, a widowed mother's allowance to carry on after the widow's allowance stops, and finally a widow's pension for those widowed at 40 or over without dependent children. The widowed mother's allowance is payable only to widows having at least one child under the age of nineteen, or to widows expecting a child by their late husband.

A married woman can get a retirement pension on her husband's contributions when he retires and draws his pension provided she is then over 60, and has herself retired, or is over 65.

Benefits are payable weekly and normally collected by pensioners from local Post Offices.

Child's special allowance. A divorced woman who was receiving maintenance of at least 25p per week for support of a child from her ex-husband, is paid this allowance on the death of the ex-husband; it is not paid where the woman remarries. The benefits are paid out of the ex-husband's contributions.

Death grant. Paid to the executors or administrators of a will or to next of kin and depends upon the age of the deceased. The benefit is paid for out of the contributions made by the deceased or the spouse, or parents where the deceased is a child.

Conclusion. The benefits we have described above are only those that are met from or depend upon the contributions made. There are many other non-contributory benefits such as industrial injury benefit, redundancy payments, guardian allowances and others. All these benefits provide a very comprehensive package and some would argue that the scope is too wide and open to abuse. The system is costly and each person must decide for himself the merits of providing a comprehensive scheme such as we enjoy.

Comparison with commercial insurance

While it is not necessary for us to consider the National Insurance scheme in any more detail it will serve to complete our discussion of it if we identify the ways in which it differs from commercial insurance operations.

(*a*) It is administered by the government through the Department of Health and Social Security.

(*b*) The rate of contributions and benefits may be altered by the government through Acts of Parliament.

(*c*) The state can, by direct grants, supplement the amount paid in by way of contributions.

(*d*) The state guarantees the solvency of the scheme.

(*e*) It is compulsory that all join the scheme, subject to certain exceptions.

(*f*) The rates of contributions vary according to class but are standard among those within each class. There is no underwriting of risks.

(*g*) No policy is issued and substantial savings accrue due to this.

(*h*) Contributions, premiums, are deducted from earnings, in most cases, at source.

(*i*) Disputes are handled by local tribunals and ultimately a National Insurance Commissioner, not through the courts.

SELF-ASSESSMENT QUESTIONS

Attempt the following questions and then refer to the appropriate paragraph to check your answer.

1. What factors influenced the move towards National Insurance?
2. Who in Britain pays National Insurance contributions?
3. How many classes of contribution exist?

4. When may a person be entitled to unemployment benefit?
5. What is the difference between the maternity grant and maternity allowance?
6. Can a married woman get a retirement pension on her husband's contributions?
7. Who administers the National Insurance scheme?
8. How are disputes handled under the National Insurance scheme?
9. Is underwriting, as we know it, used in calculating contributions to the National Insurance scheme?
10. Who guarantees the solvency of the National Insurance scheme?

CHAPTER TWELVE

The International Role of Insurance

CHAPTER OBJECTIVES

After studying this chapter you should be able to:
* outline the reasons for the international development of insurance;
* discuss the advantages and disadvantages of foreign development;
* outline the way in which foreign development has taken place and understand the restrictions to development;
* explain the importance of international insurance to the British economy.

INTERNATIONAL INSURANCE

So far, in this book, the emphasis has been firmly on the transaction of insurance within the United Kingdom. Passing reference has been made to foreign premiums when we discussed the balance of payments, but in the main we have concentrated on domestic insurance transactions.

What we must move on to look at finally is the international role which insurance plays. Britain has played a major role in the development of international insurance, in the main due to the strength and importance of London in terms of international finance and banking.

Since the start of international trading the need for insurance cover has related to risks external to national boundaries, although initially the insured was based in the country of origin of the venture and any cover required was arranged there. The risks to be insured related to goods and their means of transport. As trade developed, the trading nations established agencies and branches in foreign countries, and brought to these countries the customs of trade and commerce including insurance.

The London insurance market, although by no means the largest in premium income, is, however, the leading market of the world, and at this point it is appropriate to examine the reasons for its growth and importance.

The development of international business

During the seventeenth, eighteenth, nineteenth and early part of the twentieth centuries Britain was a great trading nation, and various explorers and merchants opened up many countries. We saw earlier how these maritime ventures led to the establishment of Lloyd's. This was paralleled by the growth of insurance companies to cope with increasing losses, mainly through fire, in Britain. The expansion of marine insurance and other classes were complementary to each other, in that when trading companies established premises abroad they insured them in the same market which was used for their UK risks—London.

As nationals of the developing countries established businesses it was natural, in the first instance, for them to follow the lead of the early settlers and seek insurance in the London market.

International trade required other help by way of finance and banking facilities, so that London developed as the leading centre for these facilities also.

The provision by Lloyd's of international news and information services was of considerable advantage to the traders and these services were expanded as a deliberate aid to their international insurance trade.

We shall look later at the style or form which the development took, but the branch offices and subsidiary companies established abroad by British insurers gave this country a unique knowledge and expertise of insurance requirements and operations worldwide.

London had become a strong and developed centre for trade, banking, finance and insurance by 1800, and it was in the nineteenth century that the greatest expansion of international insurance took place. Before looking at this development, let us consider the advantages and disadvantages of an international insurance facility.

London still survives as the leading world centre for insurance, in security, prestige and expertise if not in volume. One of the reasons for this is the manner in which British insurers met their liabilities abroad at the height of world expansion in insurance business when local companies failed. The Hamburg fire of 1842, the Chicago fire of 1869 and the San Francisco earthquake of 1906 saw the London market meeting its losses, while sectors of the German and American markets failed in the wake of these catastrophes. The reputation and security established at that time, and maintained since, have sustained our position as world leaders.

The advantages and disadvantages of international development

British insurers must have felt that some benefit could or would be derived from developing the international aspects of their business. We can identify four main advantages. Usually, however, it is the way of things in the real world that advantages are only achieved at a price, and we can also identify at least four disadvantages to international business.

Advantages

(a) The basic concept of insurance is that, by spreading risk, the effect of loss will be carried by the insuring public as a whole rather than the one individual who has the loss. We have seen in Chapter Ten that this principle can be extended from the private individual to the insurance company by way of reinsurance. By extension, it is desirable that the risks of one country be shared by others, particularly where some of the risks may be of a catastrophic nature when viewed from the capacity of one country's insurance market. The possibility of a Thames flood in London or another earthquake in San Francisco are topical examples of such catastrophes.

(b) The underwriting results of particular classes of insurance, and indeed of particular countries, tend to operate in cycles of heavy losses and reasonable profits. There is usually a time lag in the response to deteriorating claims experience, by way of stricter underwriting or higher premiums, so that from a purely national viewpoint the fluctuations in profit levels can be very severe, making financial management more difficult. Viewed internationally there are usually favourable results in some markets at the same time as disastrous ones in others. An international spread of risk by the leading insurers in each country will help to even out the peaks and troughs, thus leading to more stable markets. This is to the long-term benefit of policyholders everywhere.

(c) In any developed country there are likely to be multinational commercial organisations requiring cover on a worldwide basis. If the insurance market of the parent company is to retain as much of the premium income of that parent as possible, it is essential that staff are experienced in the risks of foreign countries and are aware of the pertaining insurance regulations. There is no better way to achieve the expertise required than to participate actively in as many countries as possible and with as wide a portfolio as possible.

(d) Where a nation has a large amount of foreign trade, it is desirable that its financial services are developed in parallel, not only to facilitate that trade, but as freestanding currency earners in their own right. We have seen how the London insurance market grew in this way and the major contribution which it makes to "invisible exports" (Fig. 9). We now see that as Japan has developed as a major trading nation, it too became a major provider of international insurance cover.

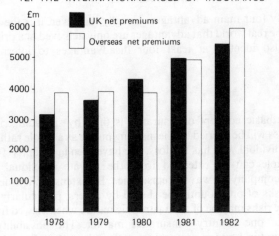

[Source: *BIA Facts and Figures*]

Fig. 9. *General business net premium income, UK and overseas (1978–82).*

Disadvantages

(*a*) Insurance companies which have been established overseas for many years are finding that the legislation being introduced is rapidly making it more and more difficult to continue operating with the same volume of business. The developing countries, in particular, are becoming more and more nationalistic in their outlook on insurance activity. Aggressive marketing by local and other foreign companies is reducing Britain's share of many markets. For prestige purposes it may be desirable to retain a presence, but at a cost to profits.

(*b*) In certain countries there is active political prejudice against foreign companies and the rates of premium they can charge.

(*c*) The same economies of scale in operating costs are not possible as at home, or as available to the national companies in the country of operation. The result is that the foreign company is less competitive.

(*d*) International development by British companies leads to the establishment of strong home-based insurers in the overseas countries. They in turn tend to expand their interests to Britain. This can have a significant effect if overseas practices and methods of reinsurance are used here, as can be seen from the American influence on the British fire insurance market in recent years.

The nature of foreign development

Having weighed all the advantages and disadvantages the insurance market must have considered that foreign development should go ahead. Over a number of years insurance companies gradually expanded their level of foreign involvement. Those who have particular interest in how this took place can find the answers in a book by H.E. Raynes, *A History of British Insurance*. For our purposes we can identify four main ways.

Home foreign departments

Home foreign departments are the head office departments of British companies, which have been established to underwrite foreign business. Where an insured or proposer has risks outside of Britain it would be this department which would consider that aspect of the overall portfolio.

This method of transacting foreign business obviates the need for, and expense of operating, a network of branches or agents overseas. In the end, however, some local expertise will be required if only to survey risks.

Overseas agencies

Another method of transacting overseas business, this time not relying on all enquiries and decisions being centralised at the UK head office, is to create a number of overseas agents. These agents could be local business or professional people who have been given authority, subject to certain limits, to issue policies and settle claims.

This system also helps to reduce the cost of establishing an overseas operation but, as with everything, there is a cost. The price the company is presumably prepared to pay is that its own qualified insurance personnel are not handling the business. Authority has been handed over to an agent.

Overseas branches

As the volume of business increases it will become less easy to handle it all through an agent, even a very efficient agent. Eventually a representation will be required in the country and this will inevitably mean a branch office. Clearly the scale of this branch operation will depend upon the volume of business written in the country, but there will be a point at which the branch becomes a more attractive alternative to either the overseas agent or the home foreign department.

Once established, the branch can become a much more effective marketing tool than either of the other two. There may, however, be areas in the world where restrictive leglislation may not allow branches of foreign companies to operate; we will look briefly at this later.

Subsidiary and associated companies

One way to overcome restrictive legislation is either to acquire a controlling interest in a local company or to come to some trading arrangement with a local company.

If a controlling interest can be obtained in a company which is permitted to transact business in the foreign country in which you are interested, then this would be a reasonable way for you to conduct your foreign business. The local company would have its own share of the market and have local expertise.

The same advantages are to be gained if it is possible for you to come to some trading arrangement with a foreign company whereby they agree to service your business in their country and you agree to service their business in your country.

Restrictions on international development

The path of international development has not always been a smooth one. The British market may have considered that advantages would result from such development and they may have designed a suitable mechanism for development, but restrictions exist and will continue to exist.

The main restriction to a company setting up operations in a foreign country is that there is often some form of state control on the establishment of foreign insurance companies. British insurers have not been nearly so successful in entering the European markets as they have others. The reasons for this are the much tighter state control which exists in European countries, the political and national changes which took place in Europe up to 1945, and keen local competition.

State control may well be desirable, and on a national basis within Europe it has been suggested that this is to protect policyholders, third party claimants, shareholders and the survival of the company. These ideas apply elsewhere in the world also. So far as foreign insurers are concerned, the controls on reserves and operations may make it impossible or impracticable for a foreign company to operate. An increasing number of countries are going further and passing legislation which prohibits the placing of insurance with companies not licensed locally. The licensing regulations may prohibit overseas companies from applying.

These latter restrictions are designed to protect and further the well-being of local insurers. It is most evident in the former British colonies which are rapidly developing and wish to develop a healthy insurance industry to support their domestic and foreign trade.

Prior to the creation of the European Community (the EEC) and the effective dates of various directives, such restrictions were also common in West Germany, France and Italy. Other countries have gone even further and nationalised their insurance industries.

While such restrictions enable local insurers to expand to the detriment of outsiders, they have some inherent dangers for the countries involved. We mentioned that international insurance operations were one method of spreading the risk to a country's national insurance market of a national disaster, or destruction of a major plant producing a country's main product. Such losses could place new national insurers, which have not yet fully developed, in serious financial difficulties.

Some countries have recognised this fact and allow international placings of reinsurance business while still restricting direct operations to local companies.

Even where foreign insurers are allowed to operate either directly or through reinsurance, there may be foreign exchange restrictions on the amount of the repatriation of funds and profits allowable per annum.

THE IMPORTANCE OF INTERNATIONAL BUSINESS

The fact that British insurers are transacting business abroad implies that premiums will flow into the United Kingdom. Before trying to gauge how important this in-flow of premiums is, let us establish the volume of business involved.

The volume of foreign business

It would be an almost impossible task to obtain premium figures from all insurers transacting business. It is just as difficult to obtain premium figures from United Kingdom insurers. Fortunately, however, the British Insurance Association does gather excellent statistical information from its (approximately) 340 member companies. These companies transact about 95 per cent of the worldwide business of the British market.

By looking at their statistics over the past five years we can build some picture of the volume of foreign business. Figure 9 (see p. 198) illustrates net premium income.

There is no determinable trend in the volume of overseas business written by British insurers, but two points are noticeable. First, the UK net premium income has steadily grown, and secondly the volume of overseas net written premiums is very close to the UK figure.

To these figures for BIA companies must be added Lloyd's premium income which for the period 1978–82 are as follows:

Lloyd's worldwide premiums
(£m)

1978	2052
1979	2245
1980	2595
1981	3942
1982	2504

(*Source: BIA statistics bureau.*)

These figures represent the total premiums received in these calendar years. In 1982, approximately 29 per cent of the total premium income of Lloyd's was made up of UK business. In other words, approximately £1,778 million was derived from overseas business. Adding this figure to the £5,836 million generated from overseas by BIA companies gives a total figure of £7,614 million of premiums relating to overseas business.

Importance to the economy

These figures on premium income do not, however, show what the country *earns* from attracting overseas business. From the total premiums written must be deducted claims and expenses, and finally any overseas investment income must be added. These overseas earnings are shown in Table I for the period 1978–82.

TABLE I. OVERSEAS EARNINGS OF THE INSURANCE INDUSTRY 1978–82
(IN £ MILLION)

	1978	1979	1980	1981	1982
Underwriting					
—companies	313	278	186	150	102
—Lloyd's	354	312	188	254	215
	667	590	374	404	317
—less earnings of UK branches of overseas companies	13	16	28	29	29
	654	574	346	375	288
Overseas portfolio investment income	148	207	264	299	524
UK brokers' overseas earnings	237	228	238	302	362
	1,039	1,009	848	976	1,174

[Source: *UK Balance of payments*, HMSO]

These figures on their own do not illustrate the importance of overseas insurance earnings. To measure that, we will have to compare these earnings with other earnings.

Let us do this comparison in two stages. First, we can compare the insurance earnings with those of other financial services, and secondly we can look at these total financial services in relation to the overall balance of payments.

Table II shows our first comparison.

TABLE II. NET INVISIBLE EARNINGS 1978–82 (IN £ MILLION)

	1978	1979	1980	1981	1982
Insurance	1,039	1,009	848	976	1,174
Banking	701	212	457	1,340	1,656
Commodity trading	295	285	340	360	449
Brokerage	248	331	370	490	481
Other	135	182	277	348	609
Total	2,418	2,019	2,292	3,514	4,369

[Source: *BIA Facts & Figures*]

These financial service earnings are referred to as "invisible" earnings and we have already discussed this in Chapter Three. From Table II it can be seen that insurance represents a significant proportion of all invisible earnings. On average, over the five years shown in the table, insurance has accounted for more than one-third of the total invisible earnings of the country.

The overall balance of payments position for the five years 1978–82 is shown in Table III.

TABLE III. UK BALANCE OF PAYMENTS 1978–82

	1978	1979	1980	1981	1982
Net trade (the difference between visible exports and imports)	−1,542	−3,449	1,233	3,008	2,119
Invisible earnings	2,418	2,019	2,292	3,514	4,369

[Source: *UK Balance of Payments*, HMSO]

In can be seen here that the balance of trade took a sharp up-turn in 1980. This was due to the increasing revenue from the exporting of North Sea oil, a phenomenon which some believe will be short-lived. However, even when oil exports are included in the figures, the amount earned by invisibles, of which we have decided insurance represents about one-third, is still greater.

What we can do now is to look at the geographical division of Britain's overseas premium earnings and then concentrate on two of our most important markets.

THE SOURCE OF OVERSEAS BUSINESS

It is extremely difficult to obtain figures which show the geographical split of premium income. This task is helped by Carter and Godden's annual book, *The British Insurance Industry: A Statistical Review*. They extract information from the published accounts of eleven major British insurers showing the source of their overseas business. These eleven companies, for 1982, represent 79 per cent of the total volume of general overseas business as shown in Fig. 9 for all BIA member companies, and hence form a useful base upon which to draw certain conclusions. Table IV illustrates the source of overseas business over the last five years.

TABLE IV. SOURCE OF OVERSEAS BUSINESS 1978–82 (IN £ MILLION).

	1978	1979	1980	1981	1982
USA	1,305 (42%)	1,288 (42%)	1,304 (44%)	1,836 (48%)	2,345 (51%)
Canada	464 (15%)	443 (14%)	431 (14%)	579 (15%)	653 (14%)
Australia	219 (7%)	198 (6%)	183 (6%)	210 (5%)	257 (6%)
Europe	654 (21%)	655 (21%)	585 (20%)	634 (17%)	695 (15%)
Others	496 (15%)	488 (17%)	482 (16%)	580 (15%)	651 (14%)
Total	3,138 (100%)	3,072 (100%)	2,985 (100%)	3,839) (100%)	4,601 (100%)

The figures in brackets show the percentage of the premium income derived from the various areas. Figure 10 shows the same figures but illustrates them in a slightly different way.

It can be seen from this diagram that the United States market is by far the largest source of overseas business. In 1982 it amounted to over half of all overseas business written by those eleven companies mentioned earlier. Europe comes next, and when Europe is added to the United States market then we can see that about two-thirds of overseas business is generated from America and Europe. This does highlight the importance of the United States and European markets and it is upon these two which we will now concentrate.

The United States market
Clearly, the United States market is extremely important. It is important both in terms of the share of the world market which it retains

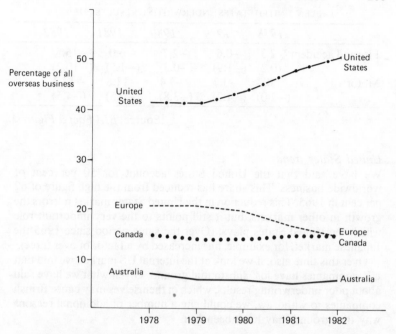

Fig. 10. *An analysis of the source of overseas business.*

and the volume of business written there by United Kingdom companies.

The United States is by far the largest single market for insurance in the world. It is difficult to say exactly what proportion of all business is accounted for by the United States, but an approximation of 50 per cent is realistic.

Given the gigantic volume of business underwritten in the United States then it is clear that the British market must be heavily involved in it. While a substantial proportion of all overseas business written by British companies is derived from the United States, this is not in itself a measure of how important the market is. To ascertain this we could look at the profit derived from the business written. If we look for example at fire and accident and motor results in the United States, we have the figures in Table V.

The figures in Table V represent the profit or loss expressed as a percentage of premium income, and so in the case of fire and accident business in 1982 there was a loss amounting to 15.5 per cent of the premium income. The figures in brackets are those for United Kingdom business only, and it can be seen that the American experience has steadily deteriorated.

TABLE V. UNITED STATES UNDERWRITING RESULTS 1978–82.

	1978	1979	1980	1981	1982
Fire and accident	2.3	−0.6	−2.7	−6.0	−15.5
	(0.2)	(−1.9)	(−0.3)	(−1.5)	(−10.2)
Motor	0.3	−3.7	−7.4	−11.8	−17.1
	(−2.0)	(−4.2)	(−3.8)	(−0.5)	(−4.5)

[Source: *BIA Fact & Figures*]

United States trends

We have said that the United States account for 50 per cent of worldwide business. This share has reduced from the high figure of 62 per cent in 1965. This reduction in the United States market mirrors the growth in other markets, but it still points to the very important role which the United States plays. (Over the same period since 1965 the Japanese market, for example, has increased by a factor of over three).

Over this time also, if we look at the internal US market, we find that UK companies have lost substantial ground. Given what we have said about poor underwriting results, which in themselves may cause British companies to withdraw, we could cite a number of additional reasons why this ground may have been lost.

(*a*) There was fierce competition from direct selling by US companies. This phenomenon is now prominent in the UK life scene. British companies may have been slow to respond to this form of marketing.

(*b*) In the 1960s several British insurers withdrew from many of the states because of alleged protection to home-based insurers by the State Insurance Commissioners. Even where these companies have returned they may well have lost ground permanently.

(*c*) Agents have the legal right to renew contracts and can switch business to obtain higher commission rates.

(*d*) US Mutuals have an excellent record for service and claims service, and not only the British companies but also many US proprietary companies have lost ground to them.

(*e*) There has been a growth in risk management risk financing techniques, and it is possible that American companies have been more willing to accommodate the requests of large buyers of insurance than have British companies.

Before leaving the United States market it is worthwhile pointing out that during the late 1970s and early 1980s links between British and United States insurance brokers strengthened. The following list shows some of the better known connections.

1978   Leslie & Godwin acquired by Frank B. Hall
1980   C.T. Bowring acquired by Marsh & Mclennan
1980   Wigham Poland 57% acquired by Fred S. James
1981   Alexander Howden acquired by Alexander & Alexander.

Here we can see that four of the US's major brokers now have transatlantic links. These links are all with Lloyd's brokers, thus giving the American broker direct access to the important market place of Lloyd's.

The European market

We saw in Table IV and Fig. 10 that Europe was a significant source of overseas business. The European share of world premiums is also significant, standing at about 25 per cent. However, the British share of this western European market has declined. This decline could be attributable to a number of causes, but in the main it would have to be said that there has been a more rapid increase in productivity on the continent of Europe than in Britain. This fact could then account for the increased volume of business generated on the continent.

Linked with this is the fact that the range of covers offered on the continent was for many years narrower than in Britain, but now this imbalance has been redressed.

SELF-ASSESSMENT QUESTIONS

Attempt the following questions and then refer to the appropriate paragraph to check your answer.

1. What are the advantages of international development of insurance?
2. Outline the disadvantages of the international development of insurance.
3. In what ways has the overseas development of British insurers taken place?
4. What are the restrictions on international development?
5. What do you understand by the term "invisible earnings"?
6. What country is the most important source of overseas business for British insurers?
7. What has been the experience of British insurers in the United States?
8. Why has the British share of the United States market decreased?
9. What factor has prompted many American brokers to become associated with British brokers?
10. Why has the British share of the western European insurance market decreased?

EXAMINATION QUESTIONS

Attempt the following questions, allowing yourself no more than 30 minutes per question.

1. Explain the importance of the doctrine of proximate cause in the investigation of insurance claims, illustrating your answer with appropriate examples.
2. Why are subrogation and contribution corollaries of indemnity?
3. What do you understand by the term "assignment" and how does assignment operate in relation to life and non-life policies?
4. What questions would you expect to find on a proposal form for private car insurance?
5. In what ways does National Insurance differ from commercial insurance?
6. What factors would an underwriter consider important when assessing the proposals for the insurance for a garage involving car sales and repairs?
7. Discuss the importance of reinsurance and the relationship between the insured, the insurer and reinsurer.
8. Discuss the advantages and disadvantages of the different ways by which a British insurance company may embark upon foreign development of its operations.

Index